"WITTY, WELL-WRITTEN,
AND ENJOYABLE"

—*Birmingham Alabama News*

". . . written with humor and deep commitment. He covers most of the things a young husband ought to know to get along with the other sex, and they are things that most of the 'marriage manuals' completely ignore."

—*Family Life*

"This book is a gem in the truest definition of the word. It is small in size but of great value for any two people who ever joined themselves in one union."

—*Durham N.C. Morning Herald*

"Dr. Shedd . . . has a clever style of putting across ideas on marriage for young people—and most refreshing of all, he doesn't moralize, preach or lecture. He speaks the language of young people."

—*Wichita Falls Times*

LETTERS TO PHILIP:

On How to Treat a Woman

CHARLIE W. SHEDD

SPIRE BOOKS

FLEMING H. REVELL COMPANY ● OLD TAPPAN, NEW JERSEY

This Jove Book contains the complete
text of the original hardcover edition.
It has been completely reset in a typeface
designed for easy reading and was printed
from new film.

LETTERS TO PHILIP

A Jove Book / published by arrangement with
Doubleday, a division of Bantam Doubleday Dell Publishing Group, Inc.

PRINTING HISTORY
Doubleday edition published 1968
Jove edition / January 1978
Special Sales Edition / April 1992

Library of Congress Catalog Card Number: 68-11400

Jove Books are published by The Berkley Publishing Group,
200 Madison Avenue, New York, New York 10016.
The name "JOVE" and the "J" logo
are trademarks belonging to Jove Publications, Inc.

PRINTED IN THE UNITED STATES OF AMERICA

DEDICATED to

MARILYN

Our first daughter-in-law,

for whom we began praying when Philip was a baby. And, from what we have observed during their first year of marriage, it is perfectly obvious that God answers prayer.

CONTENTS

PREFACE

This is for Philip. I'm sure you'd like him right off if you met him. He'd put out his hand, turn on his million-dollar grin, and give you the feeling that he is genuinely interested in what's going on inside you.

He is. From the time he took his first toddler steps, he had as many friends as there were people up and down our block. He just naturally loves folks.

He also loves Marilyn and that's where I come in. A few weeks before their marriage he asked me in his best you-can't-turn-me-down style, "Dad, would you write me some letters on how to be a good husband?"

There may have been several reasons why he would make such a request. For one thing, he knows that by the very nature of my work I spend many hours with husbands and wives who aren't making a go of it. Then, too, prior to our daughter's marriage I wrote *Letters to Karen* and every parent wants to spread his attention equally.

But there was another more important reason why Phil would ask that I do this. He needed to know! Would you believe any virile young man could grow to adulthood these days without catching on that there are two sexes? Well, if anyone could, he did! Until he met Marilyn, I don't think he had given it a second thought that God created people male and female.

This incredible situation probably started that day when he stuck his finger in an empty light socket. Most three-year-olds give it one try and learn right there this isn't for them. But not Phil. The whole event seemed to turn him on. From that day to this he's had a passion for anything with wires, current, and how does it operate?

What would you do if your son's first grade teacher called to say that Junior had been cutting classes? Well, you'd probably panic, like we did. But after the first few times, if he was like Philip, you'd do some research on where the electricians were working in the neighborhood. Then you would make your way to wherever that was and there he would be, totally enthralled in the goings-on. Or, if it was lunch hour, you might find the little guy sitting on a box bombarding the elders with questions.

If you couldn't find him, naturally you would imagine all sorts of horrible things. But after a while you would get used to that too. So you would sit on the front steps and wait. Finally, here he'd come, staggering under a load of switch boxes, insulators, wires with all those pretty-colored strands, and a multitude of broken parts with which his heroes had loaded him down.

Then you would take him back to school, all the while explaining that he must get a *general* education. You would also wonder what to answer when he'd say, "But, daddy, my teacher is so dumb she doesn't know *anything* about electricity!"

Of course, it all came out fine, like so many things do in the raising of children. He became an expert ham radio operator and greater love for his hobby hath no man than one of these. It is a perfectly marvelous thing when this happens to a boy who couldn't care less about school. They say that a youth who has lost interest in general education is headed for trouble. But they also say there is no known record of a ham radio delinquent and I believe them. He wouldn't have time for devilment if he was learning Morse Code, drawing schematics, building receivers, and talking all night to someone in Russia on twenty-meter band.

He wouldn't have time either for girls, which is why I can say without equivocation that at least one boy I know grew to adulthood with very little thought about male, female, and such incidentals.

Then he met Marilyn. At first she was just another passenger in his car on weekends. They were attending the same junior college. (Three cheers for the Navy! During nearly four years in a sailor uniform *they* convinced him that a general education was worth pursuing if he could work it in with ham radio.)

Then suddenly Marilyn became *the* passenger. But after several weeks of bumping her shins on his mobile "rig," listening to him "Calling C-Q! Calling C-Q!" she said "Ouch" one day in a voice that came through over the ham radio chatter.

That sounds like a reasonable thing to say, but right there, according to her report, he stopped the car, looked into her pretty eyes, and said, "Baby, let's have an understanding. If this goes on getting serious between us, you better learn to love ham radio because if anything goes, it won't be all this good stuff!" (From which you can see that he already had a good start on how to clarify certain issues.)

But don't worry about Marilyn. She knows a thing or two herself. If you could see their cozy little apartment today, you would know that here is one woman who has discovered her man's wavelength and how to keep the message coming on. Any girl who can accomplish the miracle of making the living room look like home *and* a ham radio haven is worth treating extraspecial.

So, that's why he asked me to write him like this. Then one day he suggested that we share these letters. Like he said, "Most of the guys I know want their marriage to be extraspecial!"

CHARLIE W. SHEDD
Houston, Texas, 1968

The First Letter:

TAKE CHARGE

Dear Phil,

The other day I saw an interesting plaque in one of our neighborhood gift shops. Some clever merchant was featuring it for Father's Day. The motto read:

WHEREVER DAD SITS

IS

THE HEAD OF THE TABLE

I hope it sells like crazy because this is one of the basic needs of every home. So, one of my first bits of advice on how to treat a woman is *"Take charge!"* For the good of your marriage, for the good of your children-to-be, and for the good of the nation's future I hope you'll read me loud and clear.

There are dozens of ways you might hear this: "Get control!" "Seize command!" "Run the show!" "Grab the reins!" "Call the signals!" "Stay at the helm!" "Steer your ship!" "Name the tunes!" "Bring 'em to heel!" "Sit on the lid!" Any variation will do provided you learn that there is a delicate line between "just enough" and "too much."

The image here is not that of a mighty potentate sitting on his throne, ruling his cowering subjects with an iron hand. This is more like a conductor standing on his box directing a symphony. Delicate, but definite! Subdued, yet powerful!

As you know, I see many marital problems from the inside. Some things you wouldn't believe. Others are downright funny. But in some the pain is awful and among the worst are those where the only right words are "Get your foot off the lady's neck, Hitler! You can never win a woman's love by applying the hobnail boot."

What I am saying is that women hate dictators, despots, tyrants, and old meanies—but they respect strong leaders.

Here are three quotes from the feminine front to show you what I mean. Number one is the word of a successful lady editor.

"All day long," she says, "I make decisions. I talk with men, deal with men, compete with men. But at night I long to be all woman. It is so good to have a man who will open the door, order the meal, and give me the feeling that I can let down now."

The next witness is a sweet little wife whose husband obviously knows what he's doing. "Once in a while"—she smiles—"Tommy sticks his chest out and says, 'Now you listen to me, squaw! Get back in your wigwam. I'm the chief and don't you forget it!'" On first hearing, you might think this borders on rough handling. But this is what she says:

"It's funny what this does. When he says it nice, I get the best feeling. You know, all secure, and like that!"

Number three is something else. This poor soul is at the opposite end of the problem. "Can you imagine how I felt?" she asks. "We were hardly home from our honeymoon when I saw clearly that Lawrence didn't need a home, he needed a nursery. Now don't get me wrong. I know every man feels like a cry baby some days and I enjoy mothering him once in a while. But all the time? When is it my turn?"

I could go on parading a long line of these.

Some good. Some bad. But none quite as sad as the weary women who can't lean because there is nothing to lean on. Their men are too weak, too careless, too preoccupied, too much at the office, too long at their cups, or too something else to be the strong male figure at the head of the house.

Of course, like everything else, there are two sides to this story. Some juggernaut types may want their men to be submissive. But I also know good women who took command because somebody had to march the troops and dad was too weak to do it.

So take it from me, your wife will love you more if she knows that you know when to stand up and say "Have no fear! Your leader is here!"

One reason why this makes a woman feel good is that she has what you might call a feminine mystique about the future.

Emotionally, most men are much more temporary than women. It is easy for us to believe that if everything is all right this minute then it's got to be fine tomorrow. But the female mind has an innate something that looks to this day and on down the road at the same time. To some extent, women judge what is happening now by the effect they think it may have on the years to come.

Since motherhood is a large part of a woman's career, she is continually measuring her man against the background of this question: "What kind of a father will he be?" So she is bound to love you more if you take charge early because you will have settled her questions about this.

On every hand she sees evidence that too many children are missing a strong authority figure. She knows some parents who are locked in a power struggle and the little ones are losing respect. She knows others where the roles are reversed, mother has won the battle, and the children are confused. Up and down the block, across town, and out in the country there are too many homes where father has abdicated and things are coming undone.

I don't need to tell you that some real psychological monsters are coming from somewhere. They are not nice to see, and any woman who cares these days is saying to herself "The world needs character. I want my children to be good citizens!" So when she looks at you as a father-to-be, what will she see? Does she smile or get a bit nervous?

You can see that all this reaches far into the future. That's why I say you mustn't delay. Take charge early and do it right.

How?

I can't tell you for sure. Nobody can. This is something you'll have to work out yourself. No two marriages are exactly alike. Because this is true, the blending of your two sets of strong points with your two sets of likes and dislikes is a unique challenge.

Yet you won't go far wrong if you shade away all the time from being a despot and move toward the idea of establishing your home as a democracy with a male head. We love our form of government partially because we feel it is a good balance between retaining some rights and delegating certain rights to other hands. And we are likely to love it most when we feel that our leaders are strong men, capable of good judgment in matters important to all.

In a sense, Marilyn has elected you to the high post of leadership in her heart and to head up your family. This gives you great authority and it is a high trust.

Don't forget that the kind of authority we're talking about here is the *authority of love!*

It seems to me that nearly every woman I know wants a man who knows how to love, with authority!

Lead on,
Dad

The Second Letter:

LEARN TO BE KIND

Dear Phil,

One day I came into my study through my private door to find a very attractive woman waiting for a visit. As I sat down in my chair, I looked across the desk and felt that something special was about to take place. It was.

"I heard you say," she began, "that you would welcome some stories about ideal husbands. So I thought you should know about Mark. I think he is perfectly wonderful and I came to tell you why.

"From the day I started to school," she continued, "clear up to college, everyone made fun of my legs. As you can see, they look like tree stumps."

Then she stood up, and they did.

You would think she might be embarrassed to talk about herself like this. Actually, I feel a little that way as I look back on the incident. But she did it all so naturally. I remember admiring her sense of composure and thinking to myself, "This is *some* woman!"

"You know how children are," she said when she sat down to continue her story. "They can be cruel. Sometimes when I was little I would cry myself to sleep. As I grew older, I laughed with them to cover up. In high school I dated some but never more than a couple of times with any one boy and you can guess why.

"When I was a freshman in college I met Mark. I liked him right away. I felt so comfortable with him. Then he asked me to go steady and I could hardly believe it. He never made one single reference to my legs. But I did. You know, looking for assurance. Then one night he took my hands in his and said, 'Frances, I want you to quit knocking yourself. I love you the way you are. The Lord gave you good, sturdy legs. They give me a solid feeling and I like it.' You know what I did," she said. "I cried.

"Then one week," she continued, "he took me home, and when I met his mother I wanted to cry again. She was a cripple. She wore a shoe that was built up and she walked with a limp. So I looked at him and he looked at me and I think I loved him right then like nobody ever loved a man before.

"Do you know," she concluded, "that was thirteen years ago and now I can honestly laugh about my legs. Can you see why I say he's wonderful? There isn't one thing in the world I wouldn't do for Mark!"

She's not kidding either, Phil, and I'm sure you will sense that she isn't. Why? Because that's how God made women. They'll do anything in the world for you if you put them at ease about their faults; build up their strong points; and reach that high level of kindness which seems to say "The blend is what I like. I love you for what you are *in total!*" This is what the psychologists call "acceptance," and you'll find it a solid fixture in every solid marriage.

Whether it is sturdy legs, a "family nose," or any other physical eccentricity makes no difference. If you are going to be safe as a "take charge" guy you better educate yourself in the art of being kind.

I used the word educate because most of us are naturally self-centered. Whether this is an ancient self-preservation instinct from way back there, or fungus off the family tree, or something else doesn't matter as much as facing the fact that we have it. Whether this comes easier for women than for men might also be open to debate. Personally, I think it's tougher for us males. But from what I have learned in my own marriage, and seen in others, there are not many questions more important than this: *"Am I willing to train myself away from selfishness toward the point where I honestly care how the other person feels?"*

Here is one more sure thing you can count on about Marilyn—like all healthy women, she has in her makeup something which can't help responding to kindness.

Deal gently, .
Dad

The Third Letter:
START AT THE MIRROR

Dear Phil,

Do you remember the night you came home from school and asked, "Dad, what good is it *ever* going to do me to remember what Macbeth say's to this babe?"

You will admit it's no ordinary question, and I couldn't think of a single intelligent answer. I'm sorry, because I did come up with some brilliant ones later. But you know how it is. Certain opportunities have only one chance. So I went blank and there went Shakespeare right out of your life.

It certainly was not that you didn't have what it took to get through senior English. It was that senior English couldn't get through you because nobody could convince you that it mattered. But ham radio did, and was I ever proud the way you put that transmitter kit together in two days and one night! (Straight, I mean, without sleep!) The man at the store said you might "mess it up permanently" if you did it alone. But you tied right into those two thousand parts and it worked perfectly the first time you turned it on.

That's how you have always been. You could do just about anything you wanted to do!

This is why I am especially glad for one thing you said when you asked me to write you. What you said was, "I want you to send me some letters, on account of I've got a lot to learn about being a good husband."

Over the years I have known many of our gender whose attitude was "If only *she* would change, things would be just dandy!"

Of course it isn't true that all the troubles will be your fault. Yet this is a fact you can count on: A wife is much more willing to face what *is* her fault if her husband has shown that he is willing to assume what is *his* responsibility.

So I am glad for your request and the way you put it. If you keep on developing this attitude, it will be a real asset in all your relationships.

One sure mark of the "take charge" man worthy of his position is the greatness of soul that can look in the mirror and say "Here's where we begin!"

Keep humble,

Dad

The Fourth Letter:

ASK HER TO HELP YOU GROW

Dear Phil,

One kind of praise from a husband is a real bell ringer in the heart of any wife. This is the kind that goes "I couldn't have done it without you!" or "I owe it all to you!" One reason why this can't miss is that the female has an innate longing to be of worth to the male. With the good ones you don't find much variance here.

Since you started at the mirror by recognizing that your part is to be a good husband, you have already put your foot on the next step up. This is where you tell your wife that you know you have faults and ask her to help you grow.

Acceptance with kindness does not mean that you must consider each other "just perfect." So you remember that there are *two* kinds of faults to be dealt with. There are those you can never remove. These you work into your love as props to the total structure. Then there are others which can be corrected and you mark yourselves as good stewards of life if you face these intelligently—together.

Naturally, this kind of thing requires a feel for the proper cadence. There are some days when we don't have the slightest hankering for self-improvement. Sometimes it takes all the strength we have just to go on breathing. Other occasions are not for analysis. These are for enjoying each other "as is." Some couples over-press. Some wives over-nag. The Lord knows I see enough top sergeant women already without adding to their corps by encouraging this in your home. But if you have conveyed the assurance that you will welcome her suggestions, she will learn to pace herself as a good wife should.

Of course you're smart enough to know that you don't begin this with the pronouncement "I accept the places where you can never be better! But there are some areas where you could improve considerably. Let us now consider together how to remake Marilyn!"

Obviously, that won't do. So as a wise husband you initiate your family fact-finding by saying something like this: "I love your accolades, but the truth is that I do have faults. Therefore, since I respect your judgment I am soliciting your help in making me a better man."

When sufficient time has passed for her to recover from the shock (both that you are *not* perfect and that she has married someone this honest), you can follow your opening salvo with another piece of news guaranteed to make her cooperate.

What you do now is to explain that *she can help you earn more* if she will take off her rose-colored glasses. They say that money talks, and this is one place she can hear it.

When she thinks this through she will realize that you're not kidding and she better not either.

I know too many men with odd habits, personality flaws, and peculiar little mannerisms holding them back. Here, for example, is a capable minister who was recently rejected for a top pulpit because he resorts to rolling his eyes up into the top of his head when he is talking with people whom he wants to impress. If you think it was a bit pica-yunish to hold him back for a reason so small, then you better believe me, it's not just the church where these things happen.

As a matter of fact, I've heard every one of the following given as excuses for not moving some man ahead in the business world: cracking knuckles, cleaning fingernails, dropping ashes, slouching, sucking through the teeth, chewing toothpicks, picking at an eyebrow, constantly crossing legs, steady patting at a wave in the hair. In the world of buying and selling—where money changes hands, or doesn't, depending on personality reaction— things like this may determine whether a man goes up, goes down, or goes on at the same old level.

This is why you may have taken a long step forward when you educate your wife to be honest. When she offers various items for your improvement, I would train myself to make the first word of reply "Thank you!" Then when you are sure you won't argue, sure you won't pout, sure you won't retaliate, you can add "I didn't know I was doing that. You and I make a great team!"

This word "team" is another sure winner. As a matter of fact, I cannot recall a single situation in marital counseling in which either party was considering separation if they felt there was *any* improvement going on between them. But I can remember dozens who gave up because they knew their relationship was getting them nowhere.

"Incompatibility" is the most popular legal description of marital breakdown. In some cases it means these two people have grown tired of telling obvious little lies to each other. Their marriage has reached a sterile dishonesty and any future is better than that.

"Home" means so many things. Home is a haven. Home is for relaxing and letting down, way down.

No front here, just "be yourself." But when home is at its best it is also a place where two people are sharing the thrill of becoming finer persons together.

There are limitless possibilities if you get your marriage moving in this direction. As we said at the beginning, a woman is so constituted that she longs to be worth something to her mate. So if you lead out by asking her to help you improve, if you receive graciously what she has to offer and thank her for it, one day she'll turn the whole thing around and ask you to help her! Why? Because she will sense that she is married to a growing man, and she will want to grow with him.

I don't need to tell you that society desperately needs folks who are pouring into the foundation the stuff of general betterment. People like this are the hope of tomorrow. You have done a great thing when you lead your marriage to the place where you can honestly say together:

"We not only aim to be good *to* each other, but *for* each other and the world."

Keep growing,
Dad

The Fifth Letter:

SEVEN GOALS FOR COMMUNICATION

Dear Phil,

In the consultation room I hear women complaining about many different things, but high on the list is failure to communicate. For some little time now I've been gathering a collection of what I call "Sayings of Lonesome Wives." Here are three of the best examples:

"You've heard of the great stone face? Well, I married it!" . . . "All I ever see of my husband at breakfast is a hand groping for his coffee from behind the morning paper!" . . . "Would you believe it? My man can go for days on one word. To be perfectly honest, sometimes he says it twice to give it a different meaning. His total vocabulary is 'Uh!' and 'Uh! Uh!' "

What they are saying is that life gets downright grim married to a man who won't talk. It is true that some husbands never shut up, but for every one of these I know several dozen who err on the silence side.

The point I want to get over today is that this is no way to treat a woman. Unless a wife is some kind of zombi, she wants to know what's going on in the mind of her loved one.

This is especially important for a man to face because his role outside the home often moves him in the opposite direction. Anyone who has ever worked knows that part of the secret is to say "Yes, sir!" when you feel like saying "You, sir, are an old goat!"

Most men accept this as a natural part of earning their living. But it isn't natural. As a matter of fact, some psychiatrists say that this wearing of masks, living behind a façade, and burying our real feeling is nothing short of slow suicide unless we have some other outlet.

Against this background the art of verbal communication in marriage takes on special significance. In one sense it is a particular kind of life insurance. But it doesn't come cheap.

For one thing, it requires specific planning and the dedication of time in your daily schedule. Most couples would never believe that "talk" is one of the simple pleasures most likely to get lost in the shuffle. But it is. Babies and business, social engagements, committee meetings, P.T.A., television, ball games, trivia, emergencies—dozens, hundreds, thousands of things are a sinister threat to the art of communication.

In premarital consultation I always ask the young lovers how good they are at verbal exchange. Almost without exception they answer "This is one of our strongest points." But some years later they come complaining "He won't talk!" "She clams up!" By these and other plaints they indicate there is no more of the babble they both loved and counted among their blessings.

You are a wise young husband if you determine that this is not going to happen at your house.

Your mother and I had a tough time opening up to each other during our first months together. This surprised both of us. We hadn't noticed that there were vast expanses of inner withholding during the years of our courtship. But there were.

As we faced the problem together it became clear that my running from ghosts and her self-containment could lead to no good. So one day we decided to look the monster head on. We agreed to at least communicate on whether we could ever communicate all the way.

In studying just that much together we stumbled onto the fact that some of the reasons for our hesitancies were long gone. (That, incidentally, is a great discovery. When you face the truth that you no longer need to be chained to your past you have taken a long leap forward.) So we pledged each other to *try* exposing a little here, a little there, by some definite rules which might have a positive effect.

This is how we came up with a simple covenant offered here in the hope that it might be helpful. You will understand this was never drawn up as a signed document. It was more like a quiet agreement. I list them for you just the way we wrote them on our hearts.

OUR SEVEN GOALS FOR COMMUNICATION

I. *We will aim to be "best friends."* Since friendship is built on time spent together we will have no less than one good visit daily with each other. We will arrange our schedule for this and keep it high on the docket of each day's business.

II. *At least once each week we will go out together.* A dinner, lunch, or any occasion to read each other's souls is time well spent. We will not let the children, or company, or the budget, or a committee meeting, or the tyranny of "the musts" and "the shoulds" crowd out the time for each other.

III. *We make it a goal to be honest all the way.* Since this requires self-honesty first we will spend some time in healthy self-analysis. By reading, studying and discussion we will seek to understand how our personal histories are affecting our marriage.

IV. *As an ideal, forty-eight hours will be our hiding limit.* But since absolute honesty cannot always meet a deadline we agree to this —if we are not yet able to shape our feelings in words, we will keep trying. We will admit that we are struggling inside and ask for continued patience.

V. *We will aim for total mercy and forgiveness.* We may question, but we will not condemn. We will seek a spirit between us where confession is heard with tenderness. We will be thankful for a place where we can face what we are.

VI. *We will respect each other's privacy.* We will not crowd or jam the works by over-inquisitiveness. Aware that what we hide may be damaging, we nevertheless extend each other the amazing courtesy of inner destruction. Because self-revelation must come from the inside we will not push.

VII. *We will remember that mystery is a blessing.* Because it takes a lifetime to close all the gaps in the most perfect relationship we will be gentle. We will love to the fullest what is given today and expectantly wait for tomorrow.

It will be obvious why we call these goals. After that first leap forward, some of the road to heaven is bound to be slow going. To let someone into your heart can be plain awful. Sometimes it is scary. It brings up things we didn't know we had, and one of these is resistance. This is the psychological term for slamming the door, running away fast, and saying "Let's forget the whole business."

This is why so few people have what it takes to make it all the way through to genuine transparency. But you can, and if you do keep it moving with a loving hand you will one day reach those high levels reserved for brave souls who have been to the depths together.

I have known more than a dozen thrilling old couples who reached their fiftieth anniversary and three who went as far as their sixtieth. They represented a wide range of income, employment, status, and influence. But they had one thing in common. Whether it was the weather-beaten farmer in Nebraska or the smooth-faced banker in one of our largest cities; the schoolhouse janitor in a crossroads town or the president of a great university—whoever he was, he and this woman beside him had learned how to share themselves with each other in total companionship.

That is a great word—companionship. It takes on added significance as the years pass. Sexual desires might fade and the need for excitement diminish. Money worries may subside and so could your other anxieties. But there is one thing that you must be sure is continually on the increase. This is the gradual opening of two hearts to welcome each other at the core of their beings. The surfacing of the real you is the secret to long life, inner health, and total communion.

Keep talking,
Dad

The Sixth Letter:

IF YOU LIKE IT, SAY SO

Dear Phil,

There are three things I aim to do every day as a husband:

1. Tell her I love her
2. Do something nice for her
3. Pay her a compliment

The truth is that this only *sounds* simple. But you try these as a regular discipline, and you will see that they "say" easier than they "do." And the toughest of these to remember may be number three.

Psychologists tell us that there are several reasons why we restrain ourselves at this point. In some cases, they say, the hesitancy comes from a basic hostility syndrome, which means that we're mad at the whole world, people are no darned good, so down with everybody! Or somehow we got the message that, since we ought to affect a little embarrassment when we receive compliments, why should we embarrass others by praising them?

But I think there may be a more basic reason why many of us husbands are stingy with kind words. This is because we're people, and the average specimen of the human species is naturally inclined to be selfish. We spend most of our time thinking about number one. We are too preoccupied with our own emotional feelings. We don't have the time, take the time, or make the time to consider what it would mean to the other person if we opened our faces to say a good word.

You can believe me, every woman worth the name is an addict for masculine approval. And the best way to let her know you approve of her is to tell her. There are all kinds of other ways to get the job done, but from the feminine point of view, voicing your likes is one of the nicest.

One reason she is bound to think so is this: Marilyn has many needs, but one of her greatest is to please you! If things are normal at your house chances are good she's thinking of you more than you're thinking of her! This is why, if you give her some pleasant things to think on, you're doing a good thing for her, for you, and for your future together.

The Bible says, "As a man thinketh in his heart, so is he." This also goes for a woman. If you give her a lovely idea of herself, that's what she will try to become. This is why it makes so much difference what you're telling her. The time finally arrives when she accepts your estimate of her as her estimate of herself. I've seen many an ordinary-looking woman grow into a lovely thing because her husband told her she was lovely. I regret to report that I have also seen some truly gorgeous women gradually fade away because they were no longer inspired from the one source that mattered most to them.

All of which leads up to six very important words:

IF YOU LIKE IT, SAY SO!

With that as a background, I give you now a few examples of compliments I've heard or used myself to good advantage.

"You're not a woman, you're a memorable occasion!" This particular one can produce—in several places—like you wouldn't believe. One place it produces is in the boudoir. Later on I'm going to write you my thoughts on sex and we'll go into greater detail at that time. I'll give you some more classic compliments for those occasions, but suffice it to say here that you would be smart to praise her body and let her know what you like about her physical makeup. This shouldn't be hard. Pick out those things that are particularly appealing and simply tell her how you feel about them. The color of her hair . . . her eyes . . . "Ah, that voice!" . . . the sweep of her shoulders . . . and you take it from there!

You can bet the family china on this—she will respond like just great, thank you, if you let her know that you think some part of her body is among nature's lovelier manifestations. I know men who attained what must be a genius rating at this because they schooled themselves well, forced themselves to get with it, and stayed right on the job till great things happened. One of these fellows is married today to a svelte thing who is of such dimensions that you wouldn't be normal if you didn't look twice. You wouldn't believe it, Phil, if you had seen them when they stood at the altar some fifteen years ago. Perhaps he had a hunch that under all that suet there was a beauty trying to escape. Some men like a challenge. They like to be heroes. At any rate, I'm telling you true, when they walked down the aisle from the altar (forgive me) I was sure that fifteen years hence she would look like a cross between the rear end of a bus and some Wagnerian soprano. It just goes to show you what wonders can be done by a man who knows what he's doing. But let's move to another kind of compliment women really go for.

"Baby, your blueberry pie is all by itself!" Do you realize, my dear boy, what a tremendous undertaking it is to serve a good meal? Planning, buying, preparing, cooking, setting the table, dishing up, and then the whole messy business in reverse when it's over. In fact, one good meal is such an accomplishment that for you to sit there, devour it, and then hurry on back to your TV game without ever saying a good word must be a mortal sin. Of course I'm not God and I don't know the answer to the old argument about whether there are major and minor evils. But I've had to get up a few meals from beginning to end, and if there *is* a difference then neglecting to compliment the wife on a good dinner must be a very major error.

There are some instances in which you'd be a fool to pass up a one-hundred percent return on your investment. This is one of them and just seven words will do: "That was a *great* meal! Thank you!"

One wise old codger gave me this interesting

slant on food and a man's compliments. "With my method," he said, "she'll snap herself out of her blue moods and never know what happened. If I see she's feeling kind of down, I ask her to get up a dinner of all the dishes she does best. Then I suggest we invite the kids over. We sit there and brag how nobody ever fried a chicken or scalloped potatoes or put together a coconut pie with the extraspecial touch Mom puts to it. By the time everybody has heaped up his plate with seconds and heaped up the praises with it, she's feeling great."

Naturally, this wouldn't work for everyone. But a man who stays alert to his woman's needs and keeps thinking can use her strong points to bless her soul. Maybe this is what the Bible means when it says, "Let her own works praise her in the gates."

Most women know what they can do well. You had better study her specialties—and how to build them into your life together.

Now we come to a compliment that is all the go at every age and without fail: *"You just go on getting better all the time!"* If you don't think it, of course, you won't say it. But if you can't find anything you feel is an improvement, you're probably either going blind or you need to get busy. *Something* about her is bound to get better than it was a few years ago, or last week, or even yesterday. This kind of compliment always wears well, but there are a couple of instances in which it is especially appreciated.

(1) When she's been struggling for a long while to improve something, to overcome a fault, or to accomplish a difficult assignment; (2) When she moves toward middle age, old age, or whenever

you sense that she senses she's not what she used to be. A woman will be forever grateful to the man who can make her believe it when he says "You just go on getting better and better."

By now you get the idea. I've given you a few special kinds of compliments worth mulling over. You will develop your own, and they are the very best. Some of these you wouldn't want anyone to know, but they do something special for both of you and they leave an especially warm feeling when you're apart.

Right there is something else your phrases of praise can do. They can give her something to remember when you're out of town, or away for the evening, or gone fishing, or just off to work. A clever husband can learn how to turn up the thermostat when he leaves so that everything is nice and cozy on his return.

I was just about to sign off when I remembered one thing more. If you ever notice her putting her back in a position to be patted; or if she has to ask you "Don't you think it becomes me?"; or if she runs to the mirror more than usual; or if in any other way the gleam seems gone from her eye, then you better get busy. It's too many "Ah's" ago since you set her heart singing.

Women are complicated creatures? Yes! But they are also simple souls who like simple things and one of the simplest they like is one of the simplest to give.

I know this isn't the best type of comparison, but it helps me to remember that Shadrach, our family airedale, will come clear across the yard for one pat on the head. The average wife is like that. She will come across town, across the house, across the room, across to your point of view, and across almost anything to give you her love if you offer her yours with some honest approval.

Hurrah for Marilyn,
Dad

The Seventh Letter:

THE POWER OF SUGGESTION

Dear Phil,

In a few moments I'm catching a plane for home. I've been up here on a speaking engagement and, like always, heading back is the best part. But I want to tell you something that happened this morning. It illustrates what I was trying to say in my last letter about the power of words to shape a woman's future.

I'd have to add now that the same thing goes for a man. When I was shaving this morning I caught myself singing, "From the land of sky blue waters comes the beer refreshing! Hamm's the beer refreshing! Hamm's beer!"

Now you know it's a fact that I try to begin my day with thoughts from a higher source than somebody's brewery. Yet the barons paid their money and their money did the job. Last night I was listening to a ball game and by constant repetition they cut this little groove in my head where they wanted it to be.

You know also that I don't drink beer. But if I did, I bet it might be Hamm's. In spite of the fact that I vowed me a vow if I ever drank beer it wouldn't be their beer, it probably would. The truth is that I can't get this silly little ditty out of my mind—"From the land of sky blue wa-a-ters."

There's my plane call!

The point I wanted to make is this: If the power of suggestion can affect us like that from a source where we couldn't care less, what do you think it would do if we heard it over and over from someone we loved?

Teetotally yours,
Dad

The Eighth Letter:

HOW TO TELL HER WHAT YOU DON'T LIKE

Dear Phil,

Let's say now that there is something you would like to change around here. You don't want to fight about it because you have a hunch that there must be some better way to handle this one.

But you have decided that you've got to get it on the table. For your own personal peace and the future of your marriage in general the time has come to declare yourself.

What do you do now?

I have a simple rule, which I pass along today as the right approach to get these little items moving. That is the crucial thing isn't it, just getting started. If you keep your head and say a prayer you can usually handle further developments as they come along. So here's the rule:

BEGIN BY TELLING HER SOMETHING YOU DO LIKE!

Suppose it's the lipstick she's been wearing lately. It really does make her look ghastly, but be assured you won't get to first base if you exclaim "Oh no! You look like a streetwalker!"

You could actually get the job done quicker, and leave her feeling good about it, if you simply told her nicely that in your opinion that particular color somewhat diminishes her natural beauty.

You will readily see that you have done a couple of good things here. You have assured her that you like the basic Marilyn and you have played to one of human nature's strongest desires. This is the hope that we will be able to make the best possible appearance. That's how the Lord made us. We all want to impress to our maximum.

You will observe that this has almost limitless possibilities. For instance, let us suppose again. Say now she is one of those modest maidens who wants all the lights off when she disrobes for retiring. Is this the time to declare "For Pete's sake, Marilyn, did you come over with the Puritans?" Or should you say something like this: "My dear, with a body like yours . . ."

Your mother says that since you are a chip off the old block you will now have fully grasped the lesson for today.

So that's about the size of it for now, except to add this: Never let anyone lure you into the trap of thinking that because she is a woman she is likely to fall for anything. It isn't so; the truth is that the female has more native intelligence about more things than the male. I hate to admit that, but, from what I've seen close up, it's the awful truth.

Yet though they may forever out-think, out-wit, out-surmise, and out-maneuver us, there are these certain places where you can get their attention every time. One of these is right here: *There isn't a woman in the world in her right mind who would flatly reject any suggestion that might solidify her relationship with the man she loves!*

Psychologically speaking we are so put together

that we are most likely to act on the advice of people if:

1. We respect the source of this suggestion as a person of wisdom (you know she thinks you're smart because you chose her).

2. We care about our relationship to this individual, and we would like to strengthen it.

3. Their thoughts for our improvement are presented in a positive manner that makes us feel good before we have a chance to feel bad.

Positively,
Dad

The Ninth Letter:

WINNING BY LOSING

Dear Phil,

We have spent a good deal of time discussing things that can be talked through. But chances are you will also have some things requiring a different approach.

Let me tell you about one very wise husband I knew and how he used a strategic retreat to accomplish his long-range goal.

It seems his wife's aunt had given them a Victorian vase that had been in the family since "Henry the something or other." He said the only way he could describe it was that it looked like somebody's ski accident. She said it looked to her like a rare and elegant heirloom. To him the colors were lurid. For her they were perfectly gorgeous. (Like I said, it was from her family.)

But whatever else it was, the thing *was* huge and that was the problem. She insisted on keeping it as the focal point in their parlor. This happened to be on one of those large, low coffee tables. It stood in the center of the room because it just didn't look right anywhere else.

For a long time this monstrosity seemed to dominate everything in their home. It also dominated their conversation. Actually he said even their evenings were built around the question "What else shall we do tonight besides argue about 'the ski accident'?"

Now this man was some thinker, so he finally caught on. By his own admission he was being a clumsy husband and getting nowhere with these tactics. So he determined to back off and probe deep.

He could do it, too. He ran a big business, with many employees and daily decisions that called for sheer wisdom. He prided himself on his ability to manage men, encourage salesmen, evaluate markets, and see the numerous sides to every situation.

After applying his thinker to "the ski accident," he decided on a plan. One night he went home and suggested that this very evening they should rearrange the living room.

"Oh no you don't!" said she. "I know what you're up to! That vase will not budge! It's a valuable piece of property, delicate heirloom, etc., etc."

But much to her surprise, he said, "Lillian, I'm sorry I've been so stubborn. I resign. Let's leave it where it is and arrange the room around it."

When she had picked herself up from the floor and recovered her strength sufficiently, they set out to accomplish just what he had planned. After all, when a man capitulates that much, a woman can hardly say "No" to a simple request like moving the furniture. Besides, she always enjoyed these times. They did it rather regularly. It was one of their favorite games.

Right here I should tell you a little more about this couple. They loved their home as few people I've known. It was beautiful. They also loved each other dearly and that was beautiful too. Their favorite pastime was sitting together after dinner—reading, talking, sometimes holding hands, sometimes saying nothing, sometimes discussing little things and big things about their day and about each other.

Now, here comes the smart part. Being the ultra in management, he maneuvered the various pieces so that "his" chair was directly opposite "her" spot on the sofa. And between them was "the ski accident" ("elegant heirloom").

He said that he sensed he might win from the very first night. In the middle of her reading, as she was wont to do, she commented, "Harry, did you read this about . . .?" Then she craned her neck to see if he was listening. He craned his, too, and assured her he was.

That's how it went for some time. Of course, he employed other "vase movers" as he called them. Sometimes he would say, "Do you know, my dear, there is nothing I like to do better than to sit here in the evening and look at you?"

"I like you, too!" she would say, peering around the vase.

Then, naturally, there were times when one of them would move from his side to her side and vice versa, so they could do what I have already told you—hold hands and things like that. On several of these journeys around the table one or the other, sometimes dragging a newspaper, nearly upset her treasure. (He vows he never did it on purpose and I suppose he didn't. This was an honorable man.)

Why didn't they move his chair? I wondered too so I asked him. He said it was on account of the light cord and because they both liked it where it was.

You've already guessed the outcome. One day, some weeks later, he came home and where do you suppose the vase was? In the dining room, on the floor, back in a corner.

He confessed that he almost made a terrible mistake. He started to say, "Oh I see you've. . . ." Then he caught himself in time. "Oh I see," he said, "you've got your hair up! That's how you wore it the first time I saw you. I like it that way."

I asked him if they ever discussed the vase again. "Heck no!" he almost shouted. "Why should we?" (It hardly seems possible to me that a man could be that noble. How could he keep from bringing it up at least once to gloat a little? But some men have more of whatever it takes to be that noble than I have.)

Anyway, I couldn't think of one reason why they should discuss it again other than to revel a bit.

I have sometimes wondered where the vase is gathering dust today. Is it in the attic, basement, or the hall closet? Knowing him, I'm sure she's the one who finally put it wherever it is. And knowing them both, I'm sure they're still sitting there in the evenings—reading, talking, and exchanging their glances with nothing obstructing. And knowing her, I'm sure she must smile sometimes and thank the Lord for a good man who could manage so much so well, but most especially that he would manage her with the deft touch of a wise husband.

I wonder who coined the phrase "I can't win for losing!" Whoever he was, he didn't know one thing. In marriage sometimes you get what you want tomorrow by yielding some ground today.

Keep thinking,

Dad

The Tenth Letter:

FRAGMENTS OF DEVOTION

Dear Phil,

Everyone agreed that Joe was a super-sorry husband. It wasn't that he drank, or gambled, or ran around with other women. But what kept the neighbors talking was the way Ann had to earn the family living. Year after year she sat behind her desk in the lumberyard office while Joe kept floundering around.

He always had the biggest plans. Any time you met him he would be talking up a storm about some fabulous new line he had just taken on. In the years when I knew them, he sold (for a short time each) fire extinguishers, vitamins, vacuum cleaners, burglar alarms, home freezers, burial insurance, mutual funds, diet aids. These he handled intermittently between what he called "my new position as official representative" (for a short time each) of a Rocky Mountain children's camp, a Midwest denominational college, a do-it-yourself course in auto repair, a novelty line of western wear, a chain of health studios, and a photography specialist in children's pictures (the kind with the pony).

So all over town they kept saying, "Did you ever see anything like it?" or, "Wouldn't you think she'd get her fill of him?" or, "Why in the world does she take such treatment?"

Then one time she had an emergency operation and in the days of her recovery I learned another thing for sure about women. This is that THE LITTLE THINGS PAY THE HIGHEST DIVIDENDS!

Being a man, I am prone to think that it's got to cost, like a mink stole, a new car, or at least three dozen roses . . . but this is not so. What a woman likes is the fragments of devotion—small items, inexpensive gifts, any humble gesture which seems somehow to say that she has what it takes to keep a man enamored. I also learned that with woman *what it means* matters a whole lot more than what it costs or how long it lasts.

How I got the message was that every day Ann welcomed me to her hospital room with a beaming report of what Joe had brought her the night before. The record went something like this:

Monday   A jigsaw puzzle from the dime store
Tuesday   The latest issue of her favorite magazine
Wednesday   Three large yellow apples
Thursday   A seventy-nine cent box of stationery
Friday   Bouquet of wild flowers (he had driven to the country to pick them)
Saturday   Some perfume from the corner pharmacy

Sunday, Monday, Tuesday, Wednesday of the next week—other little remembrances of the same variety.

"Good old Joe," she would say, "I feel so lucky the way he spoils me! He's always been like that! So thoughtful! So kind! He's a real genius at these things!"

All of which says what? Which says that a

woman will take a whole lot—people's talk, family criticism, hard work—she will put up with all this, defend her husband vehemently, and count herself lucky if she figures him for an expert in the little matters of devotion.

There are several ways you can develop this art of extra thoughtfulness. In this letter I'm going to tell you some things I have found helpful in the hope that they may aid you as you school yourself in this direction.

For one thing, *make something special of the special days*. One of the happiest couples I know celebrates in some manner on the twenty-ninth of each month. That's the day they were married and they make it "theirs" by going out for dinner; or they have some little celebration at home; or he remembers her with a gift; or she does; or they both do. If this strikes you as overdoing it, you ought to hear that husband's witness. He claims that this monthly expenditure is worth every cent it costs, and all the memory effort it takes twelve times yearly.

Engagement anniversaries, first-date anniversaries, special anniversaries; remembering these and playing them up as extraordinary will be paid back many times over out of a woman's heart. A whole host of men never give these things one extra thought, although it would make them something special in *her* eyes if they did.

Another thing to remember is that *women go for ingenuity*. The little secret things between you; the games you play in your courting; the happy surprises she wasn't expecting—these tell her many things. One thing they say is that you are putting her high on your agenda, and this has to be good. You are thinking of ways to please her, and a woman will glow inside when she knows you've secretly been planning her happiness.

Let me give you an example of one man's ingenuity and how it works to advantage in their marriage. I heard this one day at the golf course. We were discussing "golf widows" and the men were bemoaning their wives' complaints. This fellow listened them through. Then when the time was right, he said, "You never hear my wife cry, do you? The reason is we made a deal. When I play on Saturday, I take her to dinner that night. This way she's got something to look forward to. I even notice now that she feels sort of bad when I don't play!"

So maybe this is kindness with a hook in it. Agreed that he's getting something for himself by giving her something. But the fact is, she doesn't mind. She likes it. All of which means that, with a little inventiveness, life together can offer many challenges for making things nicer both ways.

Here's another little secret you will do well to keep in the forefront: *Women go for some practical devotion.*

Questions, questions: Am I assuming my share of the work load at home? Am I hurrying off to the paper, to the television, to anywhere when I could take a few minutes to give her a hand? How long has it been since I surprised her by doing one of her jobs without telling her?

A middle-aged widow gave this interesting testimony one night in my hearing. Her husband had built up considerable holding in real estate. They had a summer home, a winter home, and they had traveled far and wide. All this had given her plenty to think about. But when it came to naming her favorite memory, she told about a small thing he did when they were just starting out. "Every Tuesday night when the children were little," she said, "he would let me go shopping alone while he baby-sat." Then she concluded, "I guess nobody but a young mother would know how I feel about that."

Words are important, and so are the special little gestures of fondness. But sometimes down-to-earth loving action is exactly what is needed to get the message through that you care.

We have said before that you had better spend some time trying to think like a woman thinks. If you do, you will discover why all these things mean so much to her. One of the strangest bits of feminine logic going on in a woman's head is something I find hard to explain. The best way I can put it is that, although she wants you to feel secure with her and she wants to feel secure with you, *she still hopes that you will keep on pursuing her even after you have won her!*

The male intellect differs here in that we are likely to reason "Well, now that's done! What's next?" The female, on the other hand, doesn't think that way. With her, this is more like our family story about Bach. You remember?

This young pianist had completed her first year at the conservatory. When her old professor at home asked her what they had accomplished that semester, she answered, "Thank goodness, we finished Bach!" Whereupon the aged sage replied, "My dear, nobody ever finished Bach. You may turn Bach off, but you never finish him!"

This is how love is to a woman. The man may think when he says "I do" that he has accomplished his mission. His wife, being much wiser about these things, senses that true love has no maximum.

For those who keep opening new roads into each other's hearts each day and very often, new possibilities are forever opening up and the greatest love goes on to new greatness.

I suppose this is why I have never heard one woman complain about her husband being too considerate. I am wondering if there is any woman anywhere who ever got too much affection? I doubt it. They're not made that way. All the good ones I know have an endless capacity for devotion and tenderness and the little things.

Never quit courting,
Dad

The Eleventh Letter:

"I CAN HARDLY WAIT TO SEE YOU"

Dear Phil,

Before we go further, it might be well for me to remind you that I have a high regard for your basic integrity.

Some of these facts I'm telling you about female reactions could be downright dangerous without a wholesome sense of honor. But the fact that certain base fellows use love's secrets ignobly shouldn't keep men of character from making life interesting where it ought to be. And God knows one place where it ought to be is in husband-wife relationships.

So, here goes with another truth you have a right to know. This is that *nothing can turn a woman on quite like knowing that she turns you on.* Something inside the most lady-like lady will respond with excitement if you find her exciting.

Those husbands I know whom I count most successful put something into their love life that seems to say "How lucky can I be to live with a thrilling woman like you?"

I take it for granted that you will begin right here—be sincere! Don't ever tell a woman something she can interpret as superficial flattery. Unless it's one of those days when you're kidding each other and you both know it, you had better keep your love-making within the range of plausibility. But you can count on it that this is a wide range. If you give her only those things she can believe, you've still got plenty of room to make life interesting.

One thing she can accept as authentic is your assurance that you miss her when you're not together and that you are looking forward to being with her again. Anticipation is a big item in the most vibrant marriages. This is sure to have the feel of the real to her because you are only continuing the way you felt when you were courting.

Don't ever lose this "I can hardly wait to see you" spirit, which was such a big part of your life together before marriage. Do you remember how it was when you came home from college? You drove right past our house and hurried on to see Marilyn. Those twenty-four extra miles (when you multiply by two) meant a lot to her. They told her more than a thousand words. Your excitement kept her excited.

Too many couples let this get away. But this is unfortunate, because they have dropped one of the most certain ways to maintain the zest in their love life.

With a little practice, you can keep the enthusiasm at high pitch and it will be worth everything to both of you. All over the place there are dozens of instruments offering themselves as aids to the husband with imagination.

One of these is the telephone. Mr. Bell did a great thing for us men when he invented this little gadget. Use it often. Call her up and tell her you're looking forward to getting home. Or when your work allows, invite her to meet you somewhere. Words like this have a special ring for feminine ears: "I've got a gap in my schedule here and I'd sure like to spend it with you! Come on down and let's have a bite together." At least one woman I know can get just as excited over a hamburger and the royal treatment at lunch as she does over a dinner in one of those restaurants where the cost for two is equivalent to the monthly payment on the car.

I find it a good procedure also to check now and then on the impression I must be making when I first get home in the evening. Perhaps I am unduly aware of this because when I'm calling on parishioners I get into many homes late in the afternoon. Often while I am there, father comes home.

There are more ways to make re-entry into the family than you could possibly imagine. If the children head for the bedroom and mama starts to stiffen, you know what that means. But if the little ones go for the door and the Mrs. begins to glow, then this little drama says a whole lot. What it says is that here is a man who is good company. This man is wanted. To be wanted at home is a high aim for all of us men.

We have said before that it doesn't always take big things to get us to our goals. Sometimes the little ones matter most. So, if I were you, I would keep checking. Are you giving her the impression that you've been thinking of her with anticipation and counting on what's going to happen between you? You can do it by telephone, or cablegram, or by the simple little telegraph of a look exchanged.

Here's something else I'd learn to work into your love life. Let her catch you now and then looking at her expectantly. Or brighten your expression when you see her looking at you. These can be every bit as effective as giving her the impression that you've just floated in over the housetops to see her.

I have heard it rumored that the French are the lovers *par excellence*. This is a little verse from over there that goes, *"Je t'aime plus qu' hier moins que demain."* In our language it reads:

> I love you more than yesterday,
> Less than tomorrow!

With every nationality and in any language the spirit of that verse goes exceedingly well with women. You can take it from one who has found it is true—you do a great thing for your life together if you keep your love looking forward with high hopes.

Expectantly yours,
Dad

The Twelfth Letter:

"LATE" IS A FOUR-LETTER WORD

Dear Phil,

When the roll is called up yonder, some folks are sure to be late. Now, tardiness is *not* a greater sin for male than female, but you should know that most wives think it is.

Some of the gripes I hear in marital consultation

go like this: "He *always* keeps me waiting!"...
"We *never* get anywhere on time." ... "He thinks
he can show for dinner any old hour he pleases!"
... "Why can't he let me know when he's held up
at the office?"

These are only a few selected at random from
dozens more like them. The truth is that I've heard
just as many from men. But let's stick to our subject and see how it applies from the husband's side.

Why does it bother a woman when her man is
constantly behind time? Like almost everything
else in marriage, there are many reasons: (a) we
said in our last letter, the feminine mind thrives
on thoughtfulness; (b) being a lady, she can't help
wondering what *really is* holding you up; (c) you
used to be prompt in your courting days ... what's
the matter? ... is she slipping?; (d) do you need
vitamins? . . . minerals? . . . something else you're
not getting?; (e) dilatory men do not make good
livings; (f) many other thoughts from minor irri-
tation to major panic.

We could go on for a long while hammering
away at this theme, but the telephone is ringing
off the wall, and I've got to be going. It might even
be one of the good gals of the parish wondering
why her pastor takes so long to answer the phone.
So we'll let it go at that for this letter.

Only, I thought it might be well to remind you
that in checking over your arrival technique, you
would do well to include this thought: Most
women appreciate a man who gets there on time
most of the time and when he can't she knows
that a phone call seldom costs more than a dime.
Ten cents isn't much for a woman's peace of mind.

Don't ever forget that a contented wife who
knows her husband has been thinking of *her* feel-

ings is worth every cent of whatever it costs to be
considerate.

> Hurriedly,
> *Dad*

The Thirteenth Letter:

HOW TO TREAT A WOMAN IN PUBLIC

Dear Phil,

Do you remember the lovely compliment paid to
some saint of years gone by?

She was pure joy and she could only
create unhappiness by being absent!

After observing for twenty-one years, I'm sure
you'll agree this is an accurate description of how
your mother affects people. Of course I'm her husband and you're her son so some might say we are
prejudiced. But among even her casual acquaintances everyone knows the lady glows.

Would you believe she hasn't always been like
this? She would be the first to tell you that in the
early days of our marriage she was painfully bash-
ful. In fact, there were more times than I care to
recall when I actually felt sorry for her. She was
that self-conscious.

The man who launched this amazing transforma-
tion was Judge Evans. He was a gentle, gray-haired
barrister who lived up the street from our house,
and for some reason he took a liking to me.

The judge always knew a need when he saw
one, so in the weeks before our wedding he took
me down into his basement study and gave me the
business.

Of course I don't remember everything he said
in the several times he did this, but there was one

note he kept playing over and over. He gave me plenty to think about concerning proper deportment in every room of the house. Yet he was continually pointing to the outside door and telling me that a marriage is only as good as what happens in public.

"From marsupial to mammal," he would begin (this was one of his favorite expressions), "the average male seems to forget everything he knows about courting when he leaves his own doorstep.

"This is nothing short of stupid. Why? Because he's missing one of the best bets the Lord ever gave a man to make his wife utterly, totally, yes I would even say helplessly, in love with her husband."

You will recognize by now that the judge had the makings of a magnificent courtroom lawyer, which he was. Before he became a judge he could hold a jury spellbound, and that's what he did to me. So I listened, because I enjoyed it, but also because I knew that he knew what he was talking about. (Mrs. Evans was a little woman. She wouldn't weigh one hundred pounds with the groceries under her arm. But was she ever something! She literally shone, and that's not bad for seventy plus, which is what she had to be. He was almost eighty and they had been married fifty-eight years.)

"Since you are about to marry," he would say, "you might as well do it right. That means keep your head screwed on when you're with your woman in public."

Then he would reach for his water glass and take a slow drink, as though he was giving the truth some time to settle. When he was sure it had he would lean over his desk to deliver the clincher.

"You can take your place with the great ones," he concluded, "if you make a list of the things I've told you and keep adding to it. This takes time and takes some doing. But you better do it. You'll never be sorry if you make her think she is strictly first class in the home, and even more classy in public."

So I took him at his word and here is the list. Some of these things are straight from him the way I remember them. Others I got from observing. A few are my very own and you can improve on these. But whatever you do, promise yourself today that you will do what the judge says: "Keep your head screwed on when you're with your woman in public."

Here is the list:

1. When you enter the room, take her arm and come in smiling. If you look happy, she will, and God knows the world needs encouragement.

2. Walk proud! Act like you are thinking "How could I be so fortunate?" If you stick out your chest she will too. Most women look better that way.

3. Say something nice when you introduce her. I mean about her. This is good practice and it lifts her spirits. If you make her feel good, you feel good also.

4. When you sit down to dinner, hold her chair! Then pat her on the shoulder and smile. Keep smiling till she looks up. She'll soon catch on and it becomes a ritual. This is a very good thing.

5. When the conversation lags ask her a question! Be sure you choose one she can answer. Make

it one of her favorite subjects and always wait for her reply. Never forget, smart people make others feel smart.

6. Never, and I mean never, fuss over little points in her story. Who cares whether the roses were true pink or only a faded red? If she is all wrong, somebody else can set her straight. But not you.

7. After dinner, if you get separated, look her up once in a while. Be sure she is pleasantly situated. Tell her you missed her and is she all right?

8. When you are ready to go, hold her coat, take her arm, and open the car door for her! Not many men do and she knows it. This makes her somebody special.

9. On the way home take her hand and tell her how proud you were to have her along. A very good procedure. It pays off later.

10. Sometime when you are with her mother alone, tell *her* how much you appreciate her daughter. No woman alive could keep this to herself, and nothing does more for your wife than a compliment coming in sideways!

So there they are and I hope you will find them helpful. I've passed them along to many men, and where they put them to work I've seen them do wonders.

You need a charmer by your side? Of course you do. What man doesn't? Well, you can have one. Ten years from today, or thirty, if you do the job right you will have a wife who is strictly first class—"first class in the home, and even more classy in public."

> Wake the town and tell the people,
>
> *Dad*

The Fourteenth Letter:

HOW NOT TO TREAT A WOMAN

Dear Phil,

If I am to do a thorough job of filling your request, it will be necessary now and then to come at our subject from the back side. Under the general theme "How *Not* to Treat a Woman" I can give you some prime examples from two sources: the embarrassing personal memoirs of yours truly, and a gathering of goofs that I call my "husband-lulu" file.

From time to time in our letters I will be drawing on both of these. Here, let me present one of the prize illustrations of why women cut their wrists and drown themselves in bathtubs. It is also why they leave notes that read "Dear John, I have gone away with Herbert. Good-bye." Fortunately, that didn't happen here, but some women are made of very stern stuff.

This one was. She came into my study looking for all the world like she had just dedicated her life to getting even. The reason she looked that way is that she had just dedicated her life to getting even.

She had been in an automobile accident five days before. Some women go all to pieces at times like this. Others, bless their hearts, experience a sudden rush of good judgment. So, being one of the latter and a dutiful wife, as soon as she could, she phoned her husband.

Now what should a man do *first* if that happens? Of course, you're right! But that's not what he did. Instead, he asked, "How much damage did it do to the car?" (Well, it was a practically new Oldsmobile.)

Query number two was, "Whose fault was it?"

You know that we all sound unsure of ourselves part of the time and particularly when our nerves are shattered. So, since her answers did not suit him, he gave her explicit instructions. (Obviously, one of those guys who thinks of all the angles *except* the right one.)

His third offering was this little gem: "Listen, darling, do not admit one thing! You phone the insurance company and I'll call the lawyer. Do you understand what I mean?"

She understood.

Then, to show you that even an idiot can do some things right, he added, "Just a minute and I'll give you the insurance number!"

"Thank you *so* much!" she said. "Aren't there *any* more questions?"

"No!" he replied, "I think that about covers it!"

"Oh, *does* it?" she shouted. "Well, just in case you're interested, I'm at the hospital with five broken ribs."

Question: How can a man effectively say "I'm sorry" after a thing like that?

Answer: He can't, effectively!

Of course I suppose in his behalf it should be noted that he *knew* the accident was not fatal. Dead wives do not make phone calls.

All this was several months ago and I am pleased to report that their union is beginning to solidify once more into something resembling a marriage. He's told her a thousand times he's sorry, and you believe he means it. But to borrow a line from the psychologists' report, "The prognosis is somewhat guarded," which, in layman's language, means "If I were you, I wouldn't bet on it."

What is the lesson for today?

Lesson: *Always, without exception, every day, all week, the whole year, permanently, with no variance, and I mean one hundred percent of the time, the female of the species responds best if she knows she is number one on some male agenda!*

Naturally, the most direct way to get this across is to tell her. "Verbal assurance" is the term and there are not many wives who can get too much of it.

"Aw, but this sort of thing isn't my strong point!" How many times have I heard them say it? Meanwhile, back at the bungalow, the lady wonders. Don't let her do that. One way or another, you must get the message through that first, last, and foremost, she's number one.

So it still doesn't sound right? Okay. This doesn't need to come by way of the lungs. Women can also read sign language. Sometimes a look or a touch or a gesture is better than a thousand words.

I know one husband who got his point across this way: He never took off his hat when he came home until he kissed his wife. Even if she was on the phone, out at the clothesline, or back in the children's bedroom, he would look her up and deliver his message.

What did he do if they had company? For an answer, I quote what she told me. "One of the biggest thrills of our first year together was the time his mother came to see us. It was her first visit. When Peter came home that night, do you know what he did? He walked right past his mother and kissed me. Then he turned and kissed her. Then he took off his hat."

Without saying a word, he had let them both know how things stood. He had also established his standing with her, which was way out ahead with the great ones.

I can see you knitting your brow and wondering "How does all this 'she's tops' treatment fit in with the 'head-man' theme?" Actually, there is no inconsistency, not even a small one. They go together so well that, in the better marriages, where you see one you'll see the other. What happens is that you can be the leading man of her household *only* if she is the leading lady of your heart.

Of course she doesn't mind your giving some thought to other things. In fact, she hopes you will. She doesn't want you working with all those wires and parts and electrical currents unless you concentrate on what you're doing. But you had better convince her one way or another that these things run a poor second to her.

Like the guy who missed his cue when his wife broke her ribs, you can be a real stumble-bum if you fail to do this. Or like the man who kept his hat on, you can be a real genius if you let her know that everything else, including your mother, comes second to her!

First things first,
Dad

The Fifteenth Letter:

TREAT HER AS A PERSON

Dear Phil,

Today's story is about a rapidly rising young executive whose wife first came for help three years ago. She said that she had been watching her husband's climb and she had this queer feeling. It seemed that, as he moved toward the top, her love moved in the opposite direction. Now it was nearing the bottom and that's why she came to see me.

The whole thing was too bad, because they had an excellent start. He was devoted and she responded. They had fun, friends, and a fine future. He signed with a going company, they bought a nice house, and life was great by any measurement.

Then, like a true young comer, he began to be promoted. There was a raise in salary and then another and another. Now he was on his way and it looked like nothing could stop him. Even she couldn't, when she sensed he was heading away from things they had agreed were important.

Finally their whole life was built around his business success. Then one night something happened that prompted her seeking outside help.

He bought her a diamond necklace. It was very expensive, and you would think that any woman might thrill to its beauty. She did, too, for something like thirty seconds. But as he was fastening it about her neck, he made one of his now familiar speeches. What he said was:

"Baby, the man you live with has just been promoted to vice-president. In order that you might always remember this day, I decided to buy you this necklace. In case you are wondering as to its value, I want you to know this little dandy cost me exactly one half of my first year's salary!"

That, she said, was the sum total of his presentation. There was not one word about how much he loved her, how he appreciated her help, how beautiful she looked—nothing whatsoever, except this ode to his own ego.

(Before we go on, let me put in this little parenthesis. Whenever you buy her a gift, let *her* tell *you* how nice your gift is, while *you* tell *her* how nice *she* is!)

His next scintillating observation came in the car that night on their way to the company ball.

"You know how it is, baby! The new vice-president has to have class! They expect it! That's what they want! Then, we'll give them class, won't we? Yessir! Real class! I can hardly wait to see how they take it!"

So they waltzed and they rhumba'd and they danced the fandango. Great evening, for him. Numerous congratulations on his new position and a few on the necklace.

En route home he concluded his carnage with this monologue:

"You know what I was thinking, baby? I was thinking what an impression it made. Did you see how it sparkled under the lights? Why even old J.B. was giving it the once-over. I'll tell you what, baby, it's a symbol! That's what it is, a symbol! We're on our way and nobody can stop us! Yes sir! Just like I say, we're on our way. . . ." etcetera, ad nauseum.

That was three years ago, and she says she doesn't care now. She wants out. He says he would like to hold it together. She says that's phony, too. It may be. The other day while the three of us were viewing the wreckage, he mused, "What will they think at the company?" I'm sorry she heard that, but I guess it wouldn't matter. All these months she has felt like a billboard, until the love in her heart has just hauled off and quit.

Success! They call her "The Bitch Goddess," and that is an accurate title. She crosses the path of every ambitious man, and when you see her sway-ing skirts on the road ahead you remember I told you this is one sinister dame!

How are you going to protect yourself against this subtle danger? One way to do it is to keep saying, and meaning it, "I love you because you're you!" These are among the sweetest words ever to fall on a woman's ear. And the reason is that she wants to know that you know *she is a person, not a thing!*

Things are to use. People are to love. Be sure it's not vice versa with you.

Keep checking,
Dad

The Sixteenth Letter:

A HALF-DOZEN "NEVERS"

Dear Phil,

"Never say never again again" are the words of a song too old for you to remember, but before we leave the "how-not-to" theme, I'm going to say "never" an even half-dozen times!

Some of these are a re-emphasis of things we have already discussed and others will be sounded again as we go along. If ever you feel we should push up the record and get on with it, you can be sure that the recollection of my own clumsy mo-ments would indicate some things need repeating. I have seen these errors so often in working with troubled marriages that I know they can be too easily forgotten.

Previously, we discussed opening up to each other in verbal sharing. You will observe that most of today's items center on what not to say. Some wag put it well when he said, "God gave man a mouth that closes and ears that don't, which should tell us something." That's a good word for husbands.

So here we go with "A Half-Dozen Nevers," which I wish somebody had told me for my first years as a husband.

1. *Never point in derision to something she can't change.*

Like we have said before, it is a smart man who decides some things once and for all. One such should be his personal decision never to throw up to his woman the things she can do nothing about. You will recall the story of Frances and how her husband worked those over-sized legs into his love to win her undying respect.

Don't ever forget it. The dictionary says that sadism is "cruel abuse of others," and there is nothing more cruel than hurling hurtful words about things which can never be changed.

2. *Never criticize her in public.*

You have noticed that certain couples make a sinister little game of slapping at each other when they are in the presence of others. Here are a few sample swats I've heard lately: Husband: "Thanks for inviting us over. This is *such* a welcome change from TV dinners!" . . . Wife: "Why doesn't John fix it? That'll be the day. He doesn't know a saw from a sawhorse." . . . Husband: "You better tell *me!* Jennie could get lost with a police escort!" . . . Wife: "Did you hear that, dear? Andy bought Jean a new Buick. *He* must be doing all right!"

This trotting out each other's weakneses beyond your own door is always in poor taste. It is acutely embarrassing to innocent bystanders; it indicates that you have not been surfacing your rancor in an intelligent way at home; and the only thing it can possibly produce between you is a desire to get even.

You must remember that with women some things are standard equipment on every model. The Lord did a good thing for us men when he made them like this, *provided* we understand how it works and work it right. How it goes here is that a woman finds it very difficult to accept unfaithfulness in any form. But, thank goodness, the reverse is also true. She can't help loving more and more a man she knows is utterly dependable. Because this is so, early in your marriage you should look her squarely in the eye and solemnly swear:

"Neither by day or by night will I ever cut you down in company. Not before my family, your family, our family. Not before friends, acquaintances, strangers. When you are with me or behind your back. *Never* by wisecrack, or snide remark, or in any manner do I intend to be anything other than one hundred percent loyal!"

3. *Never compare her unfavorably with other women.*

I remember one little wife who married a widower. He was a good catch and she was glad to get him. But she got one thing she didn't like and that's why she came to see me. "What happened," she said, "was that, after we left the church, his ex-wife seemed to come alive and I'm right up to here with her. I know how she cooked, how she looked, how she walked, how she talked. In fact," she concluded, "I don't think it's going to work unless we can get him de-Helenized!"

We couldn't! I regret to report this poor man never learned that you cannot win one woman by repeated recitation of another woman's merits.

This goes for all types and every perfect creature, ex-girl friends, neighbors, other men's wives, good-looking secretaries, movie stars, that doll on the magazine cover, the one on the billboard, widows, divorcees, singles, plus your mother. They are all in it together.

One of the commonest mistakes I see on the other-woman theme is the guy who has never put his mom where she belongs. I'm glad you have such a high opinion of yours. She can cook with the best. She can also keep house. She's lots of fun and I think she's the greatest. But that's for me, not you! You have a new first loyalty now and you better be sure Marilyn knows that Marilyn is number one in your heart.

If I bear down hard on this point, it is because I have known too many men who have never been told, or else they've forgotten that you can never reshape one woman by constant comparison with another.

4. *Never drop a delayed bomb.*

These come in several types and some of them are lethal. What I have in mind here is things like this:

Suddenly telling her you don't like something she's been doing a long time. To give a woman the idea that she has been displeasing you all these years without your saying one word can be a somewhat shattering experience. If she thinks at all, she's going to be asking "What else doesn't he like?" It makes her nervous. It shakes her confidence in herself, in you, and in the future. Of course, if you just now realized that you don't like it, that's something else. But even here there is a right and wrong way to get your point across and you better be sure you learn the difference.

5. *Never go away when she is crying.*

This goes for when she's weeping inside and you know it; or when her eyes are only slightly misty; or when she cries up a river.

Whether you caused it, or somebody else, makes no difference. Tears are a time for tenderness and there is only one move to make here. That is to draw her close and tell her you're sorry.

"For goodness sake, Marilyn, grow up!" are six more words that should never cross your lips. Maybe she needs a good cry. There is therapy sometimes in tears, and especially so for a woman if she has a big, strong shoulder to cry on. She will cherish these moments forever if you let her know that you care and you want to share them with her.

6. *Never lay a hand on her except in love.*

Of course it's illegal in some places, but even where it isn't, rough physical treatment is likely to inflict permanent damage. Most wives can forgive their husbands for not being Valentino, for not being an intellectual heavyweight, for not being vice-president of the company—but the man who resorts to brute force is something else.

One thing he is for sure is a disgrace to the male I.Q. Remember the old Chinese proverb, "He who strikes the first blow has run out of ideas." So if you are ever tempted to let one fly, then go take the dog on a tour of the lamp posts; or suddenly remember an important engagement; or if you don't think that will give you enough time, then pack your Pepsodent and leave for a spell. Anything but a haymaker!

I have known too many husbands who struck their wives and then came with the broken pieces for putting them back together. Naturally, we do the best we can, but with some things you can never recover the old splendor. Some of these poor fools are sick, some are plain mean, and some have yet to grow up. But they are all terribly hard for me to work with. The reason, I'm sure, is partly my fault. I just happen to believe that, if all the men who would hit a woman were laid end to end, it would be a good thing.

That's enough for the "nevers." Tomorrow we'll take a look at "A Few Try Not To's."

Till then,
Dad

The Seventeenth Leter:

AND A FEW "TRY NOT TO'S"

Dear Phil,

Yesterday we had a look at "A Half-Dozen 'Nevers,'" any one of which could fracture your marriage. Today I'd like to run through a few matters that might not break a woman's heart, but they could give her the bends enough to affect your relationship negatively.

These are what I call my "try not to's." I pass them along in the same spirit as all these letters. Here are some husband thoughts that have been helpful at our house. In reporting them I hope you'll take what seems worthwhile into your own mind and come up with things even better for your life with Marilyn.

Remember that treating a woman right is like putting money in the bank. One day you'll be glad you did. My experience would indicate that if you make regular deposits during the early years, the years following will pay back dividends many times over. I have also observed enough real oldies close up to believe that a good union, rightly put together over the first half, can go only one way from there—better! When your joints are ancient and creaky and you begin to dodder, there could hardly be anything finer than living in a loving relationship which you *know* you helped create. You are aware that I believe in living *today* to the fullest. But it's a smart man who lifts his eyes now and then for the long look.

Practically all of these "try not to's" require some thinking ahead. For example, here is the husband who comes home one night from work and says, "I'm going to Hawaii on business tomorrow and I thought it would be nice if you would go with me." This is bound to be great, good news, and what wife wouldn't be perfectly delirious with delight? I'll tell you what wife wouldn't! The one who finds out that her husband has known about this trip for three weeks, only he forgot to mention it.

You can see what this does to her. Whether she has children to think about (baby-sitter, food preparations, school car pool, plus numberless other things known only to mothers), or whether she has only herself to get ready (clothes to select, hairdresser to see, important committee to chair, plus numberless other things known only to women without children)—you can take it from one who learned by experience—this is no way to treat a woman. Even though she counts herself lucky to have a man who wants her along; though she knocks herself out to get ready; though she finally plops on the plane exhausted; you'll have a better time, both on this trip and the last one you take together, if you try not to treat her this way!

Of course if you've only found out today that

you're leaving tomorrow, she'll make the best of it, and she can bear it partially because she knows you're in the same jam. But whether it's Hawaii, or an afternoon trip across town, or a visit upstate where she could run in on her kinfolk, or any other situation of any kind, you get the point. She'll love you more if she knows that some of your nice gestures have been well thought out with her convenience in mind.

The same applies right down to the little things, like asking her to get your best suit ready a day ahead instead of blowing your stack because it's at the cleaners when you have a crucial appointment this very morning only you forgot to say so.

Living with this absent-minded professor type must be terribly exasperating even to those saintly souls who hardly ever droop their wings. A woman is a woman, and that means she likes all the time you can give her for big deals, little deals, and all the deals in between.

Another "try not to" you'll do well to ponder is in the realm of sharing what you know which might embarrass her later if somebody knew you knew but you forgot to tell her.

For example, suppose you heard that one of your couple friends had their new baby. What if she met the proud father two days later and inquired, "How's Betty?" with nary a word of congratulations? If he knows that you know and you simply failed to pass the glad tidings along, see what you've done? You have made yourself out a first-class failure as a friend and mortified Marilyn unnecessarily. That isn't all! You've left her wondering "What else isn't he telling?" And if you repeat this faux pas regularly you leave yourself wide open for questions like "What's the matter?

Aren't they speaking?" . . . "Poor girl! It must be tough to live with a man that thoughtless."

So whether it's a new baby, or that Mrs. Logan's mother died, or that they discovered oil in the Adam's orchard, or that you heard the neighbors have smallpox, learn to make some little pigeon holes somewhere in your head for things like this and pass them along.

There are several other items on my list of "try not to's," but your own collection will be more valuable to you than mine. There *is* one more I probably should mention because I have heard so many women complain about this one. Those wives who must endure it tell me that it gets awfully old for their husbands *never* to notice the new things. New hairdo, new dress, new perfume, new negligee, new anything. I was recently discussing how to treat a woman in a study group on marriage and this subject came up. One woman who deserved better (she was rather attractive, I thought) made this comment: "If I came home driving a new Cadillac he might possibly see that. New Cadillacs cost money. But I'm telling you the truth, if I started wearing an eye patch, I doubt if he'd notice that for six weeks!"

Let's hope she was exaggerating to get her point across. But there is no kidding about this—the more observant you are, the better she'll like you.

Try not to forget that, too!

Dad

The Eighteenth Letter:

SOME MOMENTS ARE ONLY FOR HER

Dear Phil,

I'm at the office now and things have finally quieted down after one of those "woolly booger" mornings. Just talked to your mother and she sends her love.

A few letters back I referred to what I call "the embarrassing personal memoirs of yours truly." This little beaut I am about to tell you is one of these. It will take us down an important sideroad off the "people and things" theme.

What I did on this occasion was to phone your mother about midafternoon. I began with one of her favorites, like "All I wanted was to hear your voice!" or "I just saw an interesting arrangement of molecules and it made me think of you." Then we carried on from there.

Up to here, we were going great. But then, right in the middle of the flowers, I asked, "Say, has the mail come? Did we get the check from our tax return?"

Now there is nothing wrong with tax refunds. She likes them. I like them. But I had started with "*All* I wanted," remember?

So the next sound you hear is that of the great lover falling flat on his face. There was a long silence. You know how your mother is. When there is nothing to say she says nothing.

I made several attempts to get back where we'd been, but sometimes, like the Bible says, "The mouth of a fool poureth out foolishness."

It did. Having thoroughly clobbered a very nice moment, I said good-bye and did me some thinking. What I came up with was that a man can destroy some fine things by crowding. I had let my question kill my compliment.

So, it is not true that, just because you are married, anything goes. Certainly there are days when the telephone ringing—"All I wanted was to hear you"—the U.S. mail, tax refunds, and everything you're thinking, plus everything she's thinking mixes together to brighten your love.

Then there are other times when, if you're not careful, you mess the whole thing up by mixing your subjects. I wish I had the exact words to tell you how to select and distinguish. But I guess this is one of those narrow places where each must go it alone and learn for himself.

I hope you do learn it, because most women tell me it is the unimportant, over-looked items that make the difference between the great lover and just another husband. And the great ones seem to sense that *sometimes a woman likes to believe her man is concentrating exclusively on her; that he has nothing else in mind but her; that she is interesting enough to absorb him completely.*

Stay alert,
Dad

P. S.: I am sure you have already concluded that if the eager beaver in me just *had* to know about that tax refund, he could have hung up and called back later.

The Nineteenth Letter:

DIALOGUE ON MOODS

Dear Phil,

If you ever catch yourself saying "Women, I can't understand them!" don't forget to add "Thank God!" This is one of the things that makes marriage so much fun.

I have told you a number of places where you can depend on your wife's reactions. But another sure thing is that she will love you more if you learn how to handle her when she isn't dependable.

Psychologists tell us that the best climate for healthy growth is one in which we can express the entire range of our feelings. It should be an aim of your marriage to develop your relationship until you can each say what you feel like saying, do what you feel like doing, and be what you feel like being.

But don't hurry it. The total liberty to exercise one's numerous selves without restraint is another of those things you should put with your long-range goals. Unless you go at this right you might possibly tear up so much during the first twelve months it would take that many years to put it back together.

You can see we are talking about a very subtle business. Since every person is different from every other person, and because each one of us is also different on different days (years, months, weeks, hours, too) I decided to spread out for ideas. Toward this end I called together a half-dozen men who I know well enough for a bull session on marriage and moods.

These fellows earn their livings in widely divergent fields and they are personally just about as varied as six men could be. But they are all alike here—they are successful husbands.

I told them why I wanted their reactions, so they knew that part of what they said would go into a letter to you. You can see that they got right down to it, and I give you their conversation (censored slightly) as it came from the tape. I have arranged what they said in general headings and added my own thoughts in parenthesis.

Miscellaneous comments on the mood theme:

"My job is sales and I have to study my customers' moods. Seems to me it works better when

I think of my wife as one of my customers and do the same for her."

"That's the secret right there. So many times we're smart at business and stupid at home. Sometimes it hits me hard that I treat people nice all day and act like a heel with the family."

(Do you remember the old poem of unknown authorship that I taught you long ago? "There's one sad truth in life I've found, while journeying east to west:/The only folks we really wound are those we love the best./We flatter those we scarcely know, we please the fleeting guest,/and deal full many a thoughtless blow to those we love the best.")

"I think one of the big things is to have sort of a blow-off session with myself on the way home. Kind of a de-pressurizing thing. My wife seems to match her mood to mine. If I come home happy, she's happy. If I'm owly, she's owly."

"My wife is one hundred percent dependable—bitchy all the time! But after wrestling with the kids all day I'd be like that too. So it's up to me to spend some time getting *her* de-pressurized."

"Well at our house it's a matter of whoever is down pulling the other one up Sometimes it's me. Sometimes her. It's kind of an unspoken agreement. We sort of test each other to see which one has the job to do."

Interesting comments on variability in women:

"One time my wife is sharp as a lady lawyer. Next time she asks me a stupid question like 'Who wrote the autobiography of Gypsy Rose Lee?' If a fellow is smart enough to know when his wife is dumb he can get by with plenty. Tell him that. Might come in handy."

"Yeah! It's all a matter of moods. Today she wants

to cry. Tomorrow she wants to laugh. This week she's a lamb. Next week, get out of the way."

"Tell the kid it works like that in the bedroom too. One time your wife reminds you of that novel where the missionaries go around pushing brassieres for the natives. Next time she acts like something out of a French movie. You've got to know which mood they're in before you know which way you'd better be!"

Comments relative to the recognition of moods:

"Would you believe it? My wife's moods seem to be taken from the weather?"

"I read somewhere that you can tell a lot about a woman by studying her menstrual cycle. I believe it. There's one period when she can't do enough nice things for you. Then there's a few days when she wants you to baby her. If I remember this and play up to it things go better with us."

"I learned in medical school there actually are hormonal changes then that *do* cause moods. We had a rough time before I accepted this."

"My wife wears her moods, if you know what I mean! I can almost tell what's going on in her head by the way she dresses."

Thoughts on how to handle women in their moods:

"For my money, the secret is to allow her plenty of freedom. Like you say, togetherness of the best kind is built on the right kind of apartness. She needs to have some friends of her own. She ought to go some places I don't go. If I give her this kind of liberty she gets a lot of this mood stuff out of her system. She's also less possessive of me, which makes it nicer all around."

(What he is saying is that he gives her room to be herself so she gives him room to be himself. We've been over this road before, but it's worth a repeat. That's a great word for eventual oneness—room!)

"Jack, you mentioned that sometimes Alice wants to baby you. The thing in our relationship is for me not to miss those times. I think the man should be head of the house, but sometimes he needs to make like an infant. It goes better with Joan if I let her mother me once in a while. This seems to get something out of her system, and besides I like it now and then myself."

"Geraldine tends to want her own way most of the time. I used to bow my neck, but then I did some thinking. There are a whole lot of places where it really doesn't matter. So I just 'yes, yes' her on all the little things. Then when something big comes along I say 'Here's how it's going to be.' It sure goes better with us when I remember to follow that rule."

"Of course we wouldn't be for making your boy a con man, but it's a sure thing there are some tricks he better learn to play."

"Let's go back to Tom's theme about freedom outside the home, different interests, and so forth. This also goes for when you're together. Sometimes one of you wants conversation. Then there are other days when all you want is privacy, silence, no intrusion."

"The main thing with Mary Jo is for me to feel bad when she feels bad. I used to say 'Snap out of it!' That was before I got smart. Tell him to bleed when she bleeds."

"You know what I do when my wife gets to feeling bad? If I can get her in the car I drive her through the slums. Seems like seeing all those things and then coming home brings her out of it."

"Me? I take Geraldine to a comedy!"

"Works just the opposite for us. If I can find a real sad movie I take her there. Guess she gets it out of her system through other people's sadness. What do they call it? Vicarious?"

"One thing that can throw Alice into a tailspin quicker than anything is to make fun of some crazy thing she wants to do. If it's too far out of course I've got to do something, but most of the time it's better to let her go ahead. The way I got it figured is that she'll be happier if she finds out for herself that it won't work. Or how do I know, she may need to fail for her own good. Then there was this time I was sure she'd flipped and darned if she didn't come up with a brilliant idea."

"You should have certain little jokes between you that can always bring a laugh. Sometimes when you see her headed for a bad mood if you can get her laughing you can break it up."

"Any of you fellows have trouble with jealousy? That's a bad mood he better learn to handle. When we were first married I tried everything. Teasing, closing myself off, really giving her something to be jealous about! I even went to a psychiatrist. He told me I should remember she wasn't afraid of what the other woman had, but afraid of what she didn't have. He said if I would build her up with big doses of assurance this would cure it. So that's what I've been doing and it really works!"

Interesting observations, aren't they? As I said at the outset, these are all unusually good husbands. Maybe I should tell you who they are: a salesman, a vice-president of a major oil company, a postal employee, a professor of creative writing, a rancher, and a medical student majoring in psychiatry. Yet they all have this one thing in common —their wives think they are the greatest!

Yours will too if you learn how to handle her moods.

Have fun,
Dad

The Twentieth Letter:

TROUBLES ARE FOR SHARING

Dear Phil,

Doc Wilkinson gave me an important lesson about how to treat a woman. What he did was to convince me that a man better learn to share his problems with his wife at the right time—and totally.

We were riding together that night to see a lady who had frantically phoned both of us—her doctor *and* her minister. This gal wanted to be good and ready. She claimed that she was "about to depart this vale of tears." (Her words.)

I was a young pastor fresh out of seminary. Doc had stopped to pick me up, as he was often to do later because we became the best of friends.

I wish you could have known him. He had a face like the old oaken bucket, but his heart was beautiful. To my knowledge he never turned anyone down who needed help; it would probably have taken a computer to total what people owed him in unpaid accounts; and when he died it was like a familiar old tree going down outside your window. He loved people and he could read right through them. He was one of the greatest teachers of "country psychology" I have known.

He was reading me that night. I was nervous as a green rookie up to bat for the first time in spring training. "Relax preacher," he drawled. Then in his slow, deep voice he went on, "She's not going to die. We'll fix her up, you and me together. Oh I don't mean she's got no troubles. She's got plenty, but they're all imaginary."

Then he went on to spin her story. Her husband had died the year before, and Doc summed that up like this: "Though I don't like to speak disrespectful of the dead, he really ruined her."

Seems that Henry was a good man, but "he babied her something awful." Once the cholera wiped out his herd, but he never told her. If his feeders lost money he kept that from her too. The year the barn burned Doc allowed she would never have known that either except she could see it going up in smoke.

"It's a real mistake to do a woman like that," Doc contended. "Sooner or later she'll dream up allergies and headaches and even female trouble just to give her mind something to do. A woman needs drama, that's what, and if she don't get it where she should she'll get it where she shouldn't."

The years since I heard him say this have proven how right he was. I have actually seen women take to their beds for what looked like assurance that their lives really mattered. In several of these cases my mind went back to Doc Wilkinson's lesson, and, sure enough, there was an overprotective husband trying to be a hero.

The reason why I wanted you to have this letter is that I hear too many men saying "But I don't want to concern her with my problems. After all, she has enough to worry about." (They usually say this as if they were expecting some kind of medal.)

If you ever catch yourself at this or anything like it, I hope you'll do a retake. You stood one day with Marilyn and promised to share your life "in plenty *and* in want, in joy *and* in sorrow." The husband who forgets this may be in for more trouble tomorrow than he would have today if he simply opened up and gave it to her straight.

Of course there are right and wrong ways to let our sorrows be known and there will be times when a brief postponement may be in order. But the rule has got to be that troubles are for sharing, and you deny your wife a lot if you don't believe it.

For one thing, you have cut her out of that sense of partnership, which is among the deeper reasons for marriage. "Together" is one of the most beautiful words in our vocabulary and it takes on special beauty when it indicates that two people are closing the gaps between them by drawing shoulder to shoulder against all comers.

Then, too, you insult her intelligence when you don't let her help you think your troubles through. Being as smart as Marilyn is she is very likely to sense that something is bothering you. If she has to dig this out of you time after time, sooner or later she's going to be bothered with a bunch of questions coming from that place in a woman's heart where questions congregate.

"What's the matter with *me?* Doesn't he trust me?" . . . "Does he think I'm not wise enough to help him figure things out?" . . . "Is there someone else he's telling his troubles to?" . . . And so on to a real tizzy.

We both know that there are some women whose intelligence quotient is not exactly overwhelming. But if we were to trace their lack of wisdom back to its origin, we might find it was not that they were innately lacking. They were never given a chance to develop what they had.

Yet even where there is a wide gap, this can be closed by a wise husband. I have known some couples where he was brilliant and, to borrow one of your own phrases, "she didn't know from nothin'." But he found help from thinking out loud in her presence and she felt honored to be his listening post.

If you are smart in areas she isn't, she may be all the more thrilled if you take her into your confidence. She'll tuck these happy moments in a corner of her mind for later reference—"Just think, my clever, gifted husband asked *me* what I thought!"

There is one further wrong you do her if you refrain from sharing your troubles at the right time in the right way. If you come through your difficulties with banners flying and tell her about it afterward you have denied her the thrill of participation in success. Of course it's nice when friends hit it big on their own. Three cheers for them! But there is a special glow in the celebration if we feel that we made even a small contribution to their success.

So put it all together and what does it say? It says what Doc said, "It's a real mistake to do a woman like that." Strange as it may seem, in the long run sharing your unhappiness with your wife is one way to keep her happy.

"Bear ye one another's burdens,"

Dad

The Twenty-first Letter:

FIGHT THE GOOD FIGHT

Dear Phil,

In one town where I lived two rivers met. There was a bluff high above them where you could sit and watch their coming together. It was a wonderful place for lovers to park and study miscellaneous matters of communication.

I am not thinking right now what you think I am thinking. What I am wishing is that I could take you and Marilyn there and then leave you to watch those two rivers in their meeting.

You would observe that well upstream, before they united, each river flowed gently along. But right at the point of their union, look out!

Those two nice streams came at each other like fury. I have actually seen them on days when it was almost frightening to watch. They clashed in a wild commotion of frenzy and confusion. They hurled themselves head on as if each was determined that the other should end its existence right there.

Then, as you watched, you could almost see the angry white caps pair off, bow in respect to each other, and join forces as if to say "Let us get along now. Ahead of us there is something better."

Sure enough, on downstream, at some distance, the river swept steadily on once more. It was broader there, more majestic, and it gave you the feeling that something good had been fashioned out of the conflict.

A good marriage is often like that. When two

independent streams of existence come together, there will probably be some dashing of life against life at the juncture. Personalities rush against each other. Preferences clash. Ideas contend for power and habits vie for position. Sometimes, like the waves, they throw up a spray that leaves you breathless and makes you wonder where has the loveliness gone.

But that's all right. Like the two rivers, what comes out of their struggle may be something deeper, more powerful than what they were on their own.

So the first thing you and Marilyn should do about hostility is to *accept it as a natural part of life for two red-blooded young people building a home together*. Many newlyweds panic at the first indication that there may be things somebody doesn't like around here. One young bride put it like this when she wrote to describe their first quarrel. "I guess we expected the last verse of 'How Many Ways Do I Love Thee' to go on singing itself forever."

It won't. The truth is that life would be somewhat dull if it did. No small part of the zest in a good marriage comes from working through differences. Learning to zig and zag with the entanglements; studying each other's emotions intelligently; all these offer a challenge that simply can't be beat for sheer fun and excitement.

The rule you grew up under at home was "Never be ashamed of anger. It is a natural part of being a useful person. The only thing you need to regret is when you handle it badly." If I were you, I would pass that bit of philosophy along to Marilyn and make it part of your thinking together. It will be a blessing to your marriage and make you both healthier. Ulcers come from repressed ill will. So do allergies, headaches, high blood pressure, moods, nagging, infidelity, divorce, and a lot of other things you can do without.

The second thing you should do about hostility is to *work up some kind of covenant under which you will agree to settle your differences.*

You will remember that in *Letters to Karen* I set down what your mother and I call "Our Seven Official Rules for a Good, Clean Fight." We decided to make these public not because they are the last word, but because they have done so much for us. I am repeating them here with a few comments for your consideration.

1. BEFORE WE BEGIN WE MUST BOTH AGREE THAT THE TIME IS RIGHT. The Bible warns that we are foolish to say "peace, peace, when there is no peace." But it also offers us this beautiful prayer: "Set a watch before my lips. Keep the door of my mouth." I have found that an excellent petition. There are days when all she wants is tender, loving care. Then there are other times when the light of battle leaps to her eyes and you can sense that she is ready. So, unless you are totally exhausted yourself, push on back to where she has bivouacked her troops and sound the battle cry. Let her know that you love her and if what your love needs right now is war, you're ready too.

2. WE WILL REMEMBER THAT OUR ONLY AIM IS DEEPER UNDERSTANDING. One sure test for maturity is the ability to react with sympathy toward hostility sent our way. This obviously is no small accomplishment, but it should be a personal goal toward which you move at a steady pace. When some brickbat hits, our normal reaction is to look for something to throw back. But the great hus-

band disciplines himself to say "Maybe she's got a problem! How can I help her?" You can do this partially by remembering that most anger is the result of a whole lòt which has gone before. Sometimes her rage has such a long history that you actually had very little to do with it. In this sense she's not angry at you as much as she is at those whom you've recalled by whatever it is you've done. So, never ask yourself how some innocent little remark, or some insignificant act, could cause such furor. This was only the match that lit the keg where she's been stashing her frustration. What she needs now is ventilation. The big man even learns to postpone his defense until his woman has thoroughly rid herself of whatever it is that's bugging her. Some moments aren't for explanation, but for listening. One of these is when she's only half through.

3. WE WILL CHECK OUR WEAPONS OFTEN TO BE SURE THEY'RE NOT DEADLY. Have you noticed the nuclear war tacticians using the interesting term "over-kill"? What they are talking about is slaughtering more than necessary to win the war. I think that sounds an important warning for the handling of conflict at home. One thing you sure don't want to destroy is her pride. When a woman's pride is damaged, her sense of values gets warped and that lets loose a cage full of monsters. You will avoid this serious error if you *aim to attack the problem, not the person!* Any conflict between you should leave you both intact at heart. Keep always before you the thought that you're not fighting to obliterate each other. This isn't Antietam or some other struggle to death. Then make it your aim to hold the battle fires to just the right intensity. If you do this with skill, the heat you generate may serve

to warm your marriage later to a very nice temperature.

4. WE WILL LOWER OUR VOICES ONE NOTCH INSTEAD OF RAISING THEM TWO. One of the nicest things your mother taught me was that we could get the job done as well by whispering it through rather than shouting it down.

Try this just once and I think you'll like it. Obviously, this calls for considerable discipline, but you can bet it's worth the effort. Pulverizing each other with words can be good. Getting it all out is also important. But you better learn some neuter nouns, a few sterile adjectives, and certain phrases that can be interpreted several ways. The tone of your voice, and especially the volume, is something else. The tendency is for the sound to go higher and higher with the mounting ire. So, if you've got what it takes to do this, live by the agreement that you will say it softly as you say it thoroughly.

5. WE WILL NEVER QUARREL OR REVEAL PRIVATE MATTERS IN PUBLIC. We've been over this road before, but let's note another thing in passing. It's a good idea when you're quarreling to stay away from your main source of sympathy outside the home. Your best friend, fishing partner, somebody at the office, or your mother may build up your ego and assure you that anyone as fine as you just has to be one hundred percent in the clear. But there are two things wrong with running this way when you're wounded: (a) every time you tell it, you probably make it a little bit worse than it really is; (b) going to them keeps you from going to the one person you'll finally have to settle it with, namely, Marilyn!

6. WE WILL DISCUSS AN ARMISTICE WHENEVER

EITHER OF US CALLS "HALT." This, too, requires a delicate sense of judgment. If she waves even a drooping olive branch, you'd better open your arms and welcome her there. Because each person is different and every combination of individuals is unique, you must learn by trial and error your own fine line of "enough" and "too much." One couple I know does a clever thing. They have what they call "The Committee!" This is not some outside influence. It is rather their pre-agreed signal that whenever one of them says "I think we should refer it now to The Commitee," this is their moment for "cease-fire."

7. WHEN WE HAVE COME TO TERMS, WE WILL PUT IT AWAY TILL WE BOTH AGREE IT NEEDS MORE DISCUSSING. This is especially important for newlyweds. Many young couples I know operate under the delusion that *everything* has to be settled this very day. There is one thing wrong with that—it isn't so! Some questions can fall to the floor unanswered and you can still love to the maximum even if there are matters you intend to take up later for further consideration. Point to remember: *Don't try to force more unanimity than your marriage is prepared to handle at any given stage of your development!* A great husband-wife relationship does not mean that these two have reached the peak of human coalescing. It more likely indicates that they are living up to their capacity for oneness this day with the understanding that tomorrow will give them more capacity for more total togetherness.

We have said that to fight the good fight . . .

HOLD EVERYTHING! Mark Abadie just fell out of his tree house and we've got to go to the hospital. If I don't make it back here today, I'll give you a rundown tomorrow. . . .

Same evening: Here I am back at my typewriter after a rush trip to St. Lukes. The poor kid broke both heels, several ribs, and one elbow. He's really hurting.

Just last week your mother and I were sitting on our love seat watching Mark shinny up the tree and then swing by the rope straight over to the doorway. It's a scary sight, but he makes it look easy. Every time I see him, though, I say a prayer of thanks that we got you raised with no major accidents. I have yet to see the tree you couldn't climb and you could never make me believe there aren't special angels assigned to little boys. Come to think of it, I guess Mark has one too. He might have landed on his head when the rope broke and thirty-five feet is no small fall. So, like most such times, there are some things to be glad about. Being a man, I'm sure you'll understand when I say one thing I'm glad about is that it wasn't our tree house. That one must have a whole bunch of special angels.

Well, that's a long digression, but knowing you have a large measure of sympathy, I knew you'd want to be thinking of Mark. Timmy will give you a fuller account, and since he got in here, that makes another thing I'm thankful for. At nine he's already too heavy to climb many more feet up than he is years old.

But we better get back to our business. I was saying that to fight the good fight . . .
you must accept hostility as a natural part of life and you will need some rules for surfacing things you don't like.

There is another all-important consideration in fighting the good fight. This is the *offering of apol-*

*ogies, the request for forgiveness, and the assurance
that you will do your best to forget.*

These things are especially important for husbands because the words "I'm sorry" and the language of forgiveness seem more difficult for men than women. One poor wife told me recently, "My husband's idea of settling a quarrel is to put me in his sweat box until I say, 'You were *all* right! It was my fault *completely!*' The truth is," she went on, "I've just about had it! He thinks that he and God are the only perfect beings and he may even have some questions about God!"

So help me, that's what the lady said. Marriage for her is an excruciating experience. One mark of pure hell is the absence of mercy, and for this particular gal, life has become pure hell.

Remember then that the meaurement of bigness in a man is never taken at the point of a bowed neck. It is rather determined from the spot where he can unbend in true humility to pay his honest debts with these five words: "I was wrong. Forgive me."

But suppose it was *all* her fault. She really did it this time. Now what will you do? One thing you can do is to give her an opening. How about saying "I'm sorry we're having trouble. I don't like it this way. Let's stick together, what do you say?" What she will probably say is "Well, I *was* a little bit foolish myself." A woman never forgets things like this. You have opened the gate where she can come through to set the matter straight. She'll love you forever for that.

This movement-to-get-things-settled is always much more important than who started it. Tell yourself that pointing up the origin doesn't matter nearly as much as how to make things right once more. If you keep this goal before you, the day will come when you'll be stumbling over each other as though there were a prize for the person who got there first to restore the relationship.

Another test of how mature you both are is your ability to forget what you've forgiven. Or, if the offense was one of those devastating things no normal person could possibly forget, then can you put it where it belongs? Even better, can you work it into the fabric of your love to make your marriage more of a blessing to you both? You can see that to be a good husband you must work at never forgetting some things while you work at never remembering others.

Love, after a quarrel, can be a greater thing than it was before no matter who scored the most points or who brought it on. This is a law of life. All up and down the line that's how it goes. History makes it plain that people who have fought each other in one generation turn out to be the strongest allies in the next. Why? Of course it is partially because we need them and they need us now. But there is more to it than that.

After the smoke is cleared and the truce is signed, we find that all the time they are really very much like we are. They dream the same dreams, hope the same hopes, struggle just like we struggle. We learn to admire their abilities and the things we didn't know when we were fighting actually thrill us now. Always when people get rid of rancor, love comes to take its place. It opens up vast ranges for sympathy and understanding and a genuine desire to know more of what's going on.

I have a feeling that our future existence as a human race depends on this: *Can we learn methods of clearing the hostility so that we make room for the love which is always moving in?*

Do you believe the time is coming when the nations will live together in permanent peace? That will be the day, won't it? Well, it sure can't start unless it starts somewhere.

It is some goal for any couple to see their marriage as a contribution to that.

Dad

The Twenty-second Letter:

RURAL WISDOM

Dear Phil,

This is one of those days when things are jumping up and down for doing. I was about to check it off as no time for letter writing when I recalled a quaint saying about that "over-kill" theme we considered.

What it says is:

"NEVER BURN DOWN THE HOUSE TO GET RID OF YOUR MICE"

I think this says something worth pondering on the hostility theme. So do several others I found as I rummaged through my country proverb file to check the exact wording on this one.

So I'll pass these along as today's contribution to your thoughts on how to treat a woman. Knowing you, I'm sure they will turn up their own lessons as you think them through.

"ONLY A FOOL SPITS INTO THE WIND"

"NEVER THROW STONES AT A CAT ON A GREENHOUSE"

"ALWAYS STAND BEHIND A GUN AND IN FRONT OF A MULE"

"NEVER PUT YOUR WISHBONE WHERE YOUR BACK-
BONE OUGHT TO BE"

> Whimsically,
> Dad

The Twenty-third Letter:

MONEY MAXIMS

Dear Phil,

Any survey of marital problems will include money high on the list of trouble causers. There are several reasons why this is true. For one thing, every husband-wife combination brings to the marriage different concepts. One may have been brought up by parents who indulged every want. The other may be tied up inside with a poverty complex. This person might have been raised on the installment plan. Perhaps the other heard over and over "Strictly cash! Save first, then buy!" There are dozens of other differences out of your backgrounds that may need to be analyzed.

So, early in your marriage you should consider why you each think like you do and work out a philosophy for the future that you can both live with. A basic thought structure can undergird your family financially and help to secure your marriage.

Toward this end, I present here three money maxims that your mother and I have developed through the years.

Maxim 1: *Attitude counts more than amount!*

The question is not how much you have or don't have. What matters most is how you look at it. I have known some people who were financially loaded—yet they were inwardly miserable. I have known others who had very little—yet there was a song in their hearts.

Make up your mind that you're not going to be personally happy until you get control of your money. Note I didn't say "get money" but "get control." There is one whale of a difference. Getting control doesn't mean sitting like a watchdog guarding expenditures. Neither is it a matter of having big chunks to total up or to invest at six percent. What counts is that you take charge mentally of what you do have rather than vice versa. A whole lot of folks let their money manage them, direct their thinking and rule their hearts.

Some anonymous country poet puts it like this:

> It's not how well I'd be doing
> If a million should fall to my lot;
> But what am I thinking today
> About the dollar and a quarter I've got!

Maxim 2: *Live today before tomorrow!*

This one we adopted because so many people we know are operating with a delusion. They think that when they get more dollars then they will enjoy life.

I hear this often in the consultation room: "When we get the house paid for . . . the kids through college . . . a little bit more in our savings . . . one more promotion . . . when business doubles . . . and we can carpet the living room . . . or build our own swimming pool . . . or buy that summer house we've dreamed about . . . or afford fine clothes . . . or join the better clubs . . . that will be really living!"

In one sense it is easy to see why so many people fall into this trap. Every media of communication is harnessed to make us want what we don't have and be dissatisfied until we get more things. With all the gusto of an old-time evangelist, the announcer dins in our ears that we will never arrive until we drive this sports car or fly this luxury airliner to somewhere. "Be nice to number one!" "Give yourself a treat!" "You owe it to your family!" Thus the gimme' guys blather on, and before we know it we're hooked.

Of course, it's fun to look forward. Anticipation adds zest. I hope you'll adopt a savings plan and keep some goals out there ahead of you. But don't let your dreams of tomorrow sweep today and all of its pleasures off to one side.

Here are some great words for young couples from the Bible: *"This* is the day which the Lord hath made. We will rejoice and be glad in it!"

Maxim 3: *Outgo affects income!*

Sounds crazy, doesn't it, to say that one way to have more is to give more? But this is how we've found it in our marriage. With no exception, every time we increased our giving to help others beyond our own doors, some blessing followed that we hadn't expected. It has happened so often we have come to this conclusion: *The secret to family finance is to quit worrying so much about the intake and open up the outlets until they are what they ought to be.*

As you know, we have operated our family budget on this policy: "Give ten percent, save ten percent, and spend the rest with thanksgiving and praise!"

Of course it isn't true that everybody who tithes gets rich, and it isn't so that all who get rich are good givers. But it is a fact that life for us is only what it ought to be when our giving is what it ought to be.

So, if I were you, I would establish some rule

of life early in your marriage and grow in your sense of stewardship. When you see your money as a means of helping others, or for helping God help others, you have: (a) protected yourselves from the miseries of selfishness; (b) built in a guard against losing your bearings as you prosper; (c) put yourself in a position to experience one of life's greatest thrills—that of knowing many blessings because you are a blessing to many.

You are sharp enough to observe that giving in order to get is not what this is about. But getting in order to give touches the very core of life's meaning. Those who will dare to launch out at this point will find that the God of abundance is looking for places through which he can pour his riches to bless others. At the heart of His universe, He has written certain laws, and one of these is that love comes back to the lover, joy returns to the giver, and contentment at its fullest is for those whose accounts are right.

Happy spending,
Dad

The Twenty-fourth Letter:

CLOTHES, HAIR, AND MISCELLANY

Dear Phil,

In my last letter I told you certain principles your mother and I discovered together about money. Here are some thoughts on what you as a husband can do with a few dollars to give your wife that "lucky me" feeling, which makes things nice for both of you.

Let's start with *clothes*. Whatever you can allow in your budget for Marilyn's mentionables and otherwise will bring excellent returns on the investment. Every good woman goes for nice things to wear. She likes skirts, sweaters, slacks, shorts, smocks, frocks, dresses, gowns, robes, coat (winter, spring, petti-, house, rain—these are all coats), pajamas, scarves, wraps, shawls, shoes, slippers, sandals, pumps, bonnets, caps, hats, formals, informals, and so on indefinitely. She likes all these plus a lot of additional items to go on these, with these, over and under.

Some men see all this as a threat to the family exchequer. Others make friends with the whole business and use the facts to cozy up the relationship and make their marriage merrier.

There are certain "how to's" and some "how not to's" you'd better learn and remember. One is that every woman is different. Some prefer to shop alone, and if this is how it is, you see that she has time for it and send her off with a humming heart. Let her know she has full freedom to decide for herself what she likes. And when she returns, you find something nice to say about it. Even if it's downright ludicrous, you can begin with "Well, now, that *is* a hat! I can hardly wait to see you in it!" (Be sure it isn't a handbag.)

In other words, check what you are about to say long enough to be sure it will sound like you want it to sound. How you want it to sound is a bit like the Liberty Bell. You also want your words to carry the message that you believe in her even if you aren't exactly taken with her latest purchase.

Think man! You can find something to praise. If it really is awful, maybe it was a bargain and you can praise that. Women go nuts at the bargain counter, and if you don't think so keep your eyes open and you'll see. You'll also see that she responds well if you tell her she's the best bird dog you ever saw, praise her ingenuity, and pat her on the back for saving your money.

If you do give her the wherewithal to buy by herself, go by herself, choose by herself—if you give all this and a spirit that says "If you like it, I'll like it," you have done a great thing. You have let her know that you know togetherness is never compressed. You also build yourself up in her eyes. A lot of her friends don't have husbands with hearts that generous, and aren't you the nice one?

Then there are other women who like for you to shop with them. Some prefer your company on every buying occasion and others part of the time. If she's one of these for heaven's sake go willingly and not like a sheep to the slaughter. There is, incidentally, one short line I'd never forget for these forays. It's for those moments when she steps out of the dressing room and you can tell she's wondering. If you *don't* like it and you loath to see your earnings go for things like this, now is the time to say "I don't think it does you justice!" (Here we are once more at the same old rule: It isn't always what you do, it's how you do it that counts!)

It would seem that this is enough on clothes, but there is yet a bit of miscellany which might come in handy. One such is to always notice what she's wearing. Come on now, just one small thing like style, fit, color. It never ceases to amaze me how some men can remember the color of both teams' uniforms, or the color of every car in the block, or what color lipstick some new glamor doll wore at last month's office party, yet this same brilliant dullard couldn't possibly tell you the color of his wife's latest purchase or what she had on last night.

And speaking of what she wears when you go

out, remember another thing. If she asks you before-
hand what to wear, it's all right for you to tell her,
but if she has spent thirty minutes getting it on and
then she asks you, here's one more time to cogitate
before you speculate.

Another miscellany is actually one of the "nevers."
This is that you must *never* tell her you never did
like that dress she's been wearing for months (hats,
shoes, blouses, coats, hairdos—same thing!). "I always did think it was awful" constitutes one of the
poorest arrangements of words you could possibly
put together from a woman's standpoint. There is
only one way the female mind can work if you do
this. She pictures herself practically naked every
time she's worn this outfit you never did like. That
kind of feeling is enough to give any woman the
vapors. So, if you really can't stand it any longer,
then go buy something new or take her shopping
this week and tell her anyone as lovely as she is
needs a few more things for her wardrobe.

That should be enough on this except for a tip
of the hat to those small items you pick up now
and then as happy surprises. It is well to learn her
sizes. Carry them in your wallet or in your head,
and when you see something that has her name on
it, buy it. She'll love you for all these unnecessaries.
Even more important, she'll love you. The cute
little womanly trill "Oh, you didn't *have* to" is a
whole lot cuter than you think. What it means is
that she feels she's somebody special because you
did something special and *you didn't have to!*

Now, let's hear about *hair*. It may seem odd to
include this, too, in our thoughts on money, but
this is where it belongs. Most women are trained
from infancy to take great pride in their hair. They
have spent hours combing it, brushing it, rolling it,

rearranging it, and many other things we'd call "fussing" over it.

If you don't think hair means something special to women, the next time you drive across town and stop at the lights you notice how many women (particularly those driving alone) pat their hair, twist their hair, fondle their hair, and look at their hair in the rearview mirror.

My psychiatrist friends tell me this goes back to the mother-attention syndrome, whatever that means. I'm not really sure what it means, but one thing it means is that you can do great things for your life together if you: (a) notice it; (b) praise it; (c) allow her enough money to do with it whatever it is that women do at the beauty parlor.

I'm not sure about that either, except that there must be a lot of things going on in there besides hair. News, gossip, the latest on the latest is certainly one item that comes free with the washing and rinsing and drying and setting. But there's another extra they don't get elsewhere. This is the warm sensation a woman feels in her heart about a man who earns enough and cares enough and loves her enough to provide her this blessing.

Take it from me, it is a blessing. How do I know? I know because I have seen your mother go off to the beauty shop worn down, nerves on edge, beat, only to return restored and radiant. Perhaps right now you can afford this only monthly. All right—she'll look forward to that with high anticipation. But when you can, push it up to twice a month and, finally, weekly; and, whatever you do, don't muff this line. If *she* has to suggest it, you've lost it forever. If *you* remind her that you're in charge around here and she deserves it, and you insist, she'll sit there basking under the heat waves singing a hymn inside for a man so delightfully domineering. You do it and you'll see what I mean. The hairdresser is a husband's best friend!

Now here again say something when she comes home. Of course if you think it looks like a bird's nest that's another thing. But don't be too hasty. Maybe something within her is struggling for expression. Perhaps this week she's trying to impress one of her lady friends. If you look long enough, you can find some good words to say about it. Perhaps she'll frighten off salesmen or turn down some amorous neighbor, or something! The main thing is not to commit the prize blunder. This is to ignore it! Nothing gives a woman the sensation of falling from great heights quite like getting all refurbished, and then the man she lives with doesn't even notice!

There is another bit of miscellany worth mentioning on this theme. For example, you can tell a lot about some women by the way they do their hair. Changes may indicate something. They might even tell you things she's thinking that she doesn't know she's thinking but you should. I'd give it a bit of study.

Then you ought to ponder how you handle her hair. Sometimes she likes you to fondle it, sometimes to pat it, sometimes to muss it. But sometimes she wants you to leave it alone, like when she's just come from the beauty shop. Only she never wants you to overlook it, ever!

Before we close this down, there are a few other things about women and men and money that might well be added. We've already discussed giving and saving and enjoying. I have purposely said little about managing.

Different couples need different ways to keep

books, draw up budgets, handle bank accounts, and allow for expenditures. The main thing is to have some agreement. At the outset, you may need to know to the penny what comes in, what goes out, and whatever it takes to see where it all went. Perhaps who'll do the bookwork is a matter of ego for you. You earn it, by golly, so you have the right! Later on, you may want to work out some arrangement by which she manages her part, you manage your part, and another part you manage together. Then, perhaps, when your id has had the full treatment, you'll prefer to say "Honey, you take over the books, will you? I have so many important things to do!"

But however you do it, be sure you do it fairly! I couldn't tell you the number of women I've listened to who complained about their husband's double money standard. Here are a few quotes I remember:

"He buys a twenty-dollar putter and has a fit if I spend two dollars for bath oil." ... "I bought a new dress the other day and you'd have thought it was an Italian original. He really raised cain. Of course it's all right if he buys the best tailored suits. Those he needs for business." ... "He complains that I'm getting dutchy, but he won't give me one thin dime to correct the situation." ... "Before we married, he said he believed in 'share and share alike.' Then I found out what he meant. You know, like the famous horse and rabbit sausage—one horse and one rabbit!"

All this may sound a bit overdone and it probably is. But that's another thing we learn. Exaggerations usually mean that problems have been stretched way out of proportion to the way things should be. And how they should be is *fair!*

This is interesting. I was trying to think of one exception to the rule of fairness. I've known many a woman who left her man because he spent too much, drank too much, gambled too much, or even saved too much. *But I have never known one woman who left because they were poor, if he was fair when they did have it, or if she thought he would be when they got it.*

Which says what? Which says that a woman loves a man she can count on. I hope yours can count on you to be fair, to be thoughtful, to be generous, and to be smart. What that last means is that a wise husband learns to draw his wife closer by the way he handles his dollars to handle her right.

> Think, man, think!
>
> *Dad*

The Twenty-fifth Letter:

IN-LAWS

Dear Phil,

Some wag comes up with this whimsical observation: *"Behind every successful young husband there stands a surprised mother-in-law!"*

I like that because it has such an interesting twist halfway through the saying. But the fact is that in consultation I see this problem a whole lot less than I hear jokes about it. Maybe I've been lucky. Or perhaps I've been blinded by a mother-in-law relationship that is one of the bright lights of my own life.

Your grandmother, being one of the Lord's wise women, has thanked me a thousand times for taking her daughter to love, and each time she does it

I determine that much more to love her daughter more. The truth is that, if you can win your mother-in-law over to your side, she'll give you a whole lot more credit than you deserve. There is an old line that goes, "From a man she creates a god," and one place it applies is right here.

There are a couple of reasons why she does this. For one thing, when you have children of your own you'll learn that nobody stands higher with you than those who are nice to your children. So, if you're good to her daughter, you'll warm her heart every time she thinks in the direction of your house, which, for most parents, is a whole lot.

Then there is another reason why you'll have this automatic halo working for you if you are an effective husband. Every time she recites the latest about how well you two are getting along, she is simply reaffirming the fact that her daughter is a very smart girl to have chosen so well from all those suitors. And where did she get her smart? Well, everyone knows we first learn to think under our parents' influence.

So you see you have a whole lot going for you if you can get things started right. I can't tell you all the ways to do this because every situation calls for different treatment. But you won't go far wrong if you take every opportunity to tell your in-laws how much you appreciate their daughter; how thankful you are for the great job they did; you know you are reaping the benefits of their good work, etc. Believe me, parents love those who love their own, and they can't help reacting positively to this.

Sure, there may be times when the ice is somewhat thin and you had better walk circumspectly. But when that happens, keep your brains turning over, your heart sending out all the love you can manage, your mind still grateful, *and your mouth shut.*

Like I said, I am really somewhat handicapped here due to my own good fortune and because most of the in-law problems I've seen close up have been of a different type. The sticky ones I've gotten into involved how *his* mother felt about her daughter-in-law. Some of these have been downright brutal and their gory details would add very little to how anyone, male or female, should behave themselves in any relationship.

Except for these things about getting off on the right foot, I've just about shot my wad on this subject. Only, I do have one thing in my files I'd like to pass along before I sign off. It is a letter from one who knew the problem firsthand and worked it through to a good conclusion. In part, the letter reads:

In-laws are people, only they are people who have had the advantage of being close to the one you love before you came along. Right off the bat that could place you in an unpopular spot with them and vice versa.

Looking back over some of my own experiences, I would say that since in-laws are people, they should be treated as you treat other people. If you just can't tolerate them, you can be as courteous as possible when you are forced to be with them. This ought not to be impossible. If you work with people you don't like, you usually manage to tolerate them. Perhaps it might help to think of them that way while you pray for a breakthrough.

Another thing I would do is try never to initiate the negative. If they really are impossible, your mate will probably bring that up often enough to assure you that you might be thinking straight if you don't like them. In your early days together, chances are good that a few "Yes, dears" are about all that will be needed from your side. One of the main requirements is sympathy. There should be sympathy for your mate who has suffered a whole lot longer than you have with this kind of people. Then there should also be that kind of sympathy which recognizes that ugly people have ugly problems causing them to do what they do. You might get some help if you think how tough it must be to feel like they feel. Another big need is the kind of inner honesty which faces the fact that nobody likes everybody. Maybe you wouldn't like you either if you thought like they did. And if you don't like them, there's a whole lot less turmoil inside you if you take it philosophically and determine you will not be a hypocrite. The hypocrisy that pretends too much finally becomes a terrible burden. It eventually does you in because it has a million tendons reaching out to every corner of your heart. If you let their nastiness and your dishonesty about it grow underground without ever exposing it to the light, it finally destroys your peace and ends in self-hatred.

If a husband and wife can learn to share these things together at the right time in a nice way, they can usually work out some mutual means of helping each other. If they will do this, then all the people who would divide them and all the things that pull others apart can actually work the other way.

Great thinking there, isn't it? Keep still when you should, speak up when you have to, and determine together that you will make all family problems make your love stronger.

Yours for being and having good in-laws,

Dad

The Twenty-sixth Letter:

SEX—THE TWENTY-YEAR WARMUP

Dear Phil,

What I want you to see in this letter is that it takes a long time to bring a woman to her full glory sexually. The trouble with so many men is that they expect sex to be "out of this world" immediately. But sex at its greatest is something you create by careful attention as the years pass. That is why I offer you now some thoughts on how to treat a woman for maximum sex at the end of your first two decades together.

Let's begin with the all-important fact that *your woman will respond to your manliness more if you never forget that she is a woman.* In other words, you must educate yourself in the difference between the sexes.

A good starting place is to remember that female responses are generally much slower than male. Let's get specific. If you are a normal husband you will be thinking about sex a great deal more than your wife. For instance, you are reading this story in which the author uses some bedroom scene to convey his message. Immediately you begin living with the characters. Marilyn, reading the same description thinks "How nice!" or "How repulsive!" or "I wonder who will inherit Aunt Phoebe's millions?"

The same thing applies to pictures. Those gorgeous nudes and near-nudes all over the place these days may drive us wild with desire. All the while our mate, reacting like a true woman, might be thinking "Such a ridiculous hairdo!"

Ditto for what we see in the flesh. Following an afternoon at the beach we may be in a frenzy to climb into bed. What is she feeling? She may be musing "I hope I didn't get too sunburned" or "That was a fine new recipe for fried chicken" or "Didn't the children have fun?"

It isn't that sex is less important to her. In fact, the paradox is that it may be more so. We see it as a momentary blast, a great, exciting release. For her it's an all-inclusive relationship that takes in much more than what happens in the act itself.

In one sense everything we have been saying in our previous letters represents sex for a woman: kindness, compliments, the fragments of devotion, how you treat her in public, whether you noticed her new blouse, that telephone call this morning, some unexpected gift you bought her, the way you treat the children, whether you let her be herself—all these are a part of her sex life! For you it may be a biological matter of the moment. For her it's more likely to be the total union of two lives culminating right now in full expression of their belonging.

In other words, if you are typically male, sex is likely to be a dominant feature of your attitude toward marriage. Sure, there are other nice things, yet all roads lead to sex. But for her, marriage is more a totality of relationships, one expression of which is the sex act. This understanding is important for your long-range thinking. Treating her right sexually is partially a matter of re-educating your mind to understand hers.

With this background it will be obvious that *two key words for your own sex training are "restraint" and "timing."*

I have a Frenchman friend who says, "eet ees better to make luf vunce a veek for seven hours zan seven times a veek for vun hour." I have always thought him somewhat addled and a bit too lady-like. Here it seems to me he is leaning to his feminine side. But what he says is worth thinking through. He is emphasizing the point that for a woman *quality* matters more than *quantity.*

Not so for you, especially during your early days as a husband. You're making up for lost time. You have a great reserve of pent-up feeling. During your early days together, and perhaps for a long time, you'll have trouble holding yourself back. But the day should come when your mind turns to *how* rather than *how often*, and that will be the day you begin moving your marriage toward long-range improvement.

Some young husbands take it as a personal insult if their wife isn't one hundred percent enthusiastic one hundred percent of the time. Part of this may have its origin in those stories we have read where every woman in the office is some kind of nympho hardly able to wait till five o'clock to burst into flames.

Whenever you read or hear things like this you will do well to cool it with a couple of facts. One is that these tales are often put together by some sex-starved male who is getting his jollies from his fantasies. Or he may be so aberrant that the only satisfaction he can experience is via his imagination. You better remember also that these come-on girls who do toss their torsos all over the place, or over-paint or under-dress, may actually be pitiful people who have no other sex life than what you see. (I will never forget that day in the barbershop when the headlines were making a great hulabaloo about this American millionaire who had married an Egyptian belly dancer. The gang was discussing, as barbershoppers are prone to do, what this was about. Whereupon the old barber droned, "If he wanted what I think he wanted he should have married some country girl from Iowa!")

Right! Sex flaunted in public is probably nothing more than that—flaunted sex! But if you hope someday to be where the action is, then take it from me—sex at its greatest is likely to be the do-it-yourself project of a thinking husband.

There are several "timing" secrets I have observed among the experts. One is that they are willing to let half pleasure go for full pleasure later. They know that in even the best marriages there will be ups and downs. Sometimes all a wife wants is to be left alone. So? So the *wise lover* learns to control his exuberance while the *fool* proceeds full steam ahead. By forcing the issue he gets what he wanted tonight. But what does that prove? To himself it may prove his virility. But what does it prove to her? If it only proves to her that he's selfish, or a bore, he hasn't gained one thing—he's lost a whole lot!

Another thing the wise husband knows is that nobody gets the same results every time. So this particular session was something less than a wow. What does he do now? He refuses to panic. He tells himself that there will still be high-voltage days and other nights to go native.

Then, too, the expert at love recognizes that a woman can enjoy sex in an entirely different way from her man. Let me share with you here something a young wife said to me in consultation. She had come for help because her husband was one of those pushers who kept insisting that there was only one manner of sex satisfaction, namely his!

What she said was, "I wish he would quit pressing me to get as excited as he does. I could enjoy it so much more if he would let me enjoy the closeness while he enjoys the excitement. Is it so wrong for me sometimes to think of sex purely as my ministry to his needs? Must I *always* feel like he feels?"

The right answer is a great big resounding "No!" Yet even some of the marriage manuals stick to the premise that a man is something less than all man unless he can bring his wife to climax every time.

In my experience as a counselor I'd have to take issue with their assumption. I know that there are numerous happy marriages where the wife, at least part of the time, gets her thrills from thrilling her husband. If you do badger your woman at this point you may drive her into a frustration that can only work one way—negative. Rule: Never let *your* neurotic needs take precedence over *her* feelings!

Freedom to express your desires is a great goal, but, for the first twenty years, remember it's more goal than reality. Sure an uninhibited sex life is what you want. But you won't get it by crushing her ideas of how it should be with your ideas of how it should be. The eventual aim is total freedom to experiment and let yourself go. There are infinite variations in a full sex life and numberless approaches. The fact is that *nothing you do in marriage is wrong provided it doesn't hurt either member to the union physically or emotionally*. But that last word is loaded. Unless you bring her along slowly you may destroy more in one night than it would take years to recover. So the wise husband paces himself with infinite tenderness! He moves toward harmony, slowly. He knows that with some things it isn't how much or how often, but how well. Sex is one of these!

Here is another thing the good lover knows. *He is aware that he can warm his woman with words before he even lays a hand on her.*

I am not talking here about the fact that you must let each other know what you like and don't like sexually; the things you are feeling; the thoughts you are thinking. What I would like to convey is the stimulating power of language properly used as a part of good foreplay in sex.

I once asked a group of women to write down their thoughts on compliments. Some amazing things turned up. I suppose it was because they were doing this anonymously, but several included their favorite phrases of praise from the bedroom.

Out of more than fifty entries I pass along here one solid note of warning, which appeared several times, and a few sure winners.

Warning: Women resent compliments if the only ones they hear are sex gimmicks. Here are some proofs to the point:

"How can men be such unimaginative morons? The only time my husband tells me I'm nice is when he wants sex." . . . "Whenever he get rhetorical, I know what's coming." . . . "He never flatters me unless we're in bed." . . . "My husband has a string of what I call 'bedtime lyrics.' Just once I wish he would tell me I'm nice without an ulterior motive."

That sound you hear may be a snort from the grave of Casanova. No expert lover would make such stupid mistakes. Tell yourself repeatedly that you must avoid anything that smacks of "using" rather than loving. The surest safeguard, obviously, is to praise her biscuits and her housekeeping; how well she manages your money; how nice she looked at the party; the new apron she made; and anything else you like about her.

Sex for a woman is one of those ultrasensitive things in which it is almost impossible to hide false motives. Therefore, if you want your sex life to rank with the best, you'd better keep checking to be sure that sincerity is a big part of the total relationship.

Now let's turn to some sure winners.

One woman wrote: "I think the little secret compliments you have together mean more to a woman than anything else. I love those intimate assurances that I have been thrilling to my husband!"

Some of the more daring entries prove that this lady thinks like a true woman.

"Sometimes when we are done making love my husband says, 'I, too, have lived!' That's my favorite." . . . "One of his cutest compliments is, 'Whenever I look at you in that, it's like all my evil thoughts put together in one!'" . . . "Would you believe it? Sometimes he reads me The Song of Solomon before we make love. Times like these mean everything to me."

Note how these center on a man's assurance that he is being satisfied. This is terribly important to a woman. Not only does she want to feel that she is fulfilling the basic female function of pleasing her mate, but she loves to know that he will be carrying lovely memories to feed back into his thoughts.

While we're talking about language and things to say, it is well to touch also on what shouldn't be said. If I were you I would put away forever from my vocabulary such words as "frigid," "cold," or anything frosty that you might be tempted to hurl in a moment of letdown. As we have said, a woman has a way of becoming what you tell her she is. The language you use also has twenty-year ramifications.

Guard your words for propriety. Modesty is terribly important for some. Others react favorably to a sprinkling of "earthy" expressions. Some girls are terribly naïve. Others have heard too much. If I were you I would give some thought to the vocabulary of sex. You make a serious mistake whenever you build up defenses in her at any point, where you should be leaving thoughts of high expectation.

While we're on the praise and propriety theme be sure you make a swing by the store occasionally on your way home. How about some bewitching *odeur* or a gossamer wisp of something? A small remembrance like this now and then may be just the thing to back your words. You've got to save money someplace, but one place never to do it is on women's lingerie. Make your purchase and rhapsodize. Even with the high cost of beefsteak she'll love you for such extravagance.

Before I sign off let me remind you again what we've taught you at home as the basic fact about sex. This is that *sex is a gift of God and there is absolutely nothing negative about it when it's right.*

That, I'm sure you have discovered, is much easier to say than to practice. For more than twenty years the negative has been hurled at you from all points of the compass. All these things have left their imprint. Sometimes your imagination went wild and you wondered if you weren't one of the devil's angels with sex where your brains ought to be.

Then you met Marilyn and you *knew* that was good. But here, too, there was negative in the positive. You fought to control yourself and it was one grim battle for sure.

At last you were married! Great day! Suddenly it was legal! You were free to let yourself go. But there were still these old hangers-on, and how can a man view as all-good what he has been fighting as half-bad? The answer, of course, is that it will take time and patience and a gradual reorientation of your attitudes and hers.

So that's your aim. In my judgment it is one of the highest goals any husband can set for himself. To train yourself in the art of total manliness is a noble undertaking. To educate the woman you love in full expression of her womanliness, well, that's a privilege too great to describe in words.

I wish you the best. If you do give it your best, beginning right now, and stay with it carefully for something like twenty years, the time will come when you will know what the Bible means when it says, "male and female created he them... and God saw everything that he had made, and, behold, it was very good."

Keep the home fires burning,
Dad

The Twenty-seventh Letter:

INFIDELITY

Dear Phil,

It is late, but before I go to bed I want to tell you something I heard this evening. It follows hard on the heels of what I wrote you today about sex.

This man phoned while we were having dinner

and he had to see me right then. So we met at our appointed spot and it was plain to see he was hurting.

He wasted no time getting to his problem. Before I could ask him the usual questions about family, business, or even "What's up?" he began pouring out his story.

Same song, next verse! Anyone who counsels with people hears it over and over and over—and you've already caught on. The poor devil *was* in serious trouble. His wife found out today that he is "playing around" (his words). When he arrived home this evening, there were his bags on the front step. She had packed them thoroughly and attached a note. His hand shook as he handed it to me. What it said was that she was through; tomorrow she would see a lawyer; she didn't care if she never laid eyes on him again; she would do all she could to fix it so he'd never see the children. She also said she hated him and, for all she cared, he could "drop dead!"

He was totally shattered. My heart went out to him. It always gets me to see a grown man cry and this was no exception. He admitted he had it coming. She had caught him in a carefully laid trap and was there anything I could do?

Time was when I thought the right thing at times like this was a sermon on the text "Be sure your sins will find you out." But that day is long gone. When a man confesses his guilt that freely, what he needs is an ear to hear him through; a hand to help him put the pieces back together; and a couple of feet headed in the direction of his house to see if she'll reconsider. She usually will if she is given some time to get her temperature down. When her rage subsides, the road looks terribly desolate as she sees herself going it alone with the children. Then, too, she begins to ask herself some questions about her place in their marriage and is she partly responsible?

So, I'll wait for a hunch that this is the hour and then I'll move in. You add your prayers to mine that we can get this nest back up there where it belongs.

But the things he kept saying that I wanted to pass on were these agonizing cries from deep inside: "How could I be such an ass? I don't blame her. I don't hate her. *But I sure do hate me!*"

In all my counseling with adulterers, it seems to me that this shame turned in on oneself is the major penalty. This is why the man who admits his guilt needs no lecturing from me. He'll give himself the full treatment, and it's pure hell for the fellow whose conscience is jumping up and down on his broken spirit. Of course if he won't admit it, that's something else. But even the refusal to come clean is often only a smoke screen to avoid facing the terrible truth.

This is how we are. When we were put together, our Creator wrote certain irrefutable laws in the heart of us men. One of these is that wrong must first be settled with Him before it can be made right elsewhere. No matter how we try to dodge it, the truth is that what we think of ourselves matters more in the long run than what other people think. This includes friends, enemies, employers, employees, neighbors, kinfolk, "the boys," "those guys," other women, and irate wives. We can go to the ends of the earth, or a million other places, to put distance between ourselves and anyone else. But because we are made as we are, we can never, ever, get away from us!

They say it is possible for a man to kill his conscience. But do you think he can? I've met a few who seemed to have that job done. Yet for each of these I've known dozens who had only pushed it so far down inside they simply couldn't hear it any more. Then one day it pushed over the tombstone where they thought they had buried it permanently. And from what I've seen there is nothing worse than these inner voices of integrity whispering, shouting, leering "Boo, remember me?"

This has to be one of the worst features of infidelity. No matter how much a man rationalizes his position, he knows he has taken a route that leads *away* from the real problem. He may be looking only for biological release. He may be getting sympathy from the other woman, which he doesn't feel from his wife. It may be that he is simply swept up in the excitement of clandestine amour. There may be numerous other satisfactions. But somehow they can never balance his failure to work things out right where he knows he should. He's failed at the one place where he wanted to succeed, and *this depreciates his opinion of himself*. He has taken the coward's way out, and men don't like cowards. At the heart of any male worthy of his name is the knowledge that great victories don't come cheap.

The further down life's road you go, the more you will learn that discipline, commitment, and plain, old-fashioned, manly guts are no small part of the thrill of living. The real prize comes only to the man who works things through until he can stand at the mirror and say, "Well, it wasn't easy! But I like what I see looking back at me."

It was foolish of me to overlook this part of the sex theme when I wrote you earlier today. The reason, you will realize, is a compliment to you. It never even crossed my mind that you would take the easy way. Knowing you as I do, I'm sure you'll work things out right where they should be worked out. But as I look back honestly on my own days of early marriage, I realize there were lots of things in my head that surprised and bothered me. Being a chip off the old block, the same thing may happen to you. It does to a lot of fellows. In fact, I've known plenty of men well enough to know that this is actually standard equipment on some of the best models.

When a man marries, he ties himself up to one woman because he has decided that she has what he wants, what he needs, what he longs for. Then, of all the crazy things—other women are still attractive. Maybe his sex life with his chosen isn't everything he thought it would be. Or, perhaps it is just great, thank you! Yet his mind continues to wander. There are still good-looking legs besides his wife's, and other feminine forms going by with devastating allure. Sometimes his thoughts are enough to make him wonder. Is he some kind of freak, maybe the number-one evil mind of all creation?

He isn't! Neither are you. You're a red-blooded, all-American, virile youth, and the more you're getting at home, the more thoughts of sex may be right up there at the fore in your head, your veins, your whole being!

So, what can you do about it? I mean after you accept it as natural and see it as a real challenge to your total manhood, what can you do?

One of the finest things you can do is to share your struggle with Marilyn. With me, inner battles shared with the person I love most are already half won. It was a great realization for me when I caught on to the fact that part of the perfect sex relationship is to be honest about everything, including the part that bamboozles a man and makes him feel like something out of the jungle.

Of course you must go at this right and pace the whole thing properly. But you can believe me, good women brought along carefully, have a wonderful facility for sharing these things. Even though they do not feel the sex urge like we feel it, they are equipped with something that enables them to understand male tendencies if we give them a chance. The woman who truly loves her man wants to know what he's thinking—all of it.

Your mother is a real ace at this, and I have a feeling Marilyn will be too if you do your part. One way to do it right is to develop your own honest versions of whatever it takes to get this message through: "All roads lead home! Thank you for being so great that all the interesting people I meet make me want to hurry back to where you are."

Then when you convince her that this is authentic, you can develop a nice little game between you. In it she says what she thinks and you do. She encourages you to talk freely about types you prefer, who you find interesting, what turns you on, and the whole bit. She has nothing to fear now. Neither do you. Your marriage is one of the rare ones where nobody hides, and, oh boy, how healthy!

Sex at its best is based on truth. At its best it is a spiritual relationship in which body, mind, and soul respond honestly with a song of praise to the Creator, who loves you so much that He made you to love each other.

This kind of sex is beautiful. It is holy. But it is also fun, and I hope for you that no small part of the fun will be developing things at home so you won't need to go elsewhere, because the real thing is right there, and nothing could be finer.

Faithfully,

Dad

P. S. One of the nicest things your mother ever did for me was shortly after we began sharing all these things. From somewhere she dug up this old proverb and wrote it on my heart:

God doesn't keep the birds of temptation from flying over our heads. He only asks that we keep them from building nests in our hair!

Nice, isn't it? And it is so good to know that this is how it is.

The Twenty-eighth Letter:

"EXCEPT THE LORD BUILD THE HOUSE"

Dear Phil,

One of the ancient Bible writers suggests that God is like a man with a lantern, going through time, looking for a people on whom he can build his kingdom. Our hope for you and Marilyn is that he might one day say, "I've been looking for you a long time."

Even a quick glance down the road of history makes it plain that no civilization has qualified to date. Bleaching bones all over the place are solemn evidence that lots of people who thought they had it made didn't.

Do you suppose any race of men will ever get the job done? If so, how? One way we can be sure it won't come is like a lucky row of numbers on a bingo card. Strength of character doesn't develop by chance.

So where is our hope? Is it in churches more honest and up to date, finer schools, new forms of government? Will the kingdom come when our economy is finally balanced? Does it wait for an end of poverty, second-class citizenship, war? Or does it depend on greater technology, faster space craft, some fresh new influences from beyond our own planet?

Doubtless some combination of all these influences will be part of the eventual answer. But you can put me down as one who believes that *when life is finally what it ought to be, the major source of man's new greatness will be the home.* I'll put my money on this possibility—that the Kingdom of God will come when the family is all it should be and marriage between the sons and daughters of the Lord has reached its full potential.

It does make sense, doesn't it? This is the place of our earliest influence. Over a normal life span most of us put in a major portion of our time at home. We experience our most intimate relationships there. From this base we learn most of our habits, develop most of our emotional reactions, make our first decisions on values. Small wonder poets tell us that this is life's number one shaper of destiny. It is.

What I hope I have given you here is the feeling that how well you succeed in your marriage may have an effect far down into eternity.

Yet a serious study of marriage these days does make us wonder. There are too many breaks in what ought to be solid, and cracks that shouldn't be.

Why does this happen? Nearly one hundred percent of those with whom I stand at the altar expect to live happily ever after. When they promise to cherish each other forever they really mean what they say. But one day the honeymoon ends and there are bills to pay and dishes to do and bosses to please and floors to scrub and more bills and more dishes and more bills and "Egad! Did you see this bill for insurance?" and she's talking about a new dishwasher and "Who spent $10.90 at the drugstore?" and "Why does he just sit there watching his stupid game, never making one move to help me with these dishes?"

So, this is the *real* ever after? What became of his sweet talk and where did her glamor go and "Why should I work so hard if he's not going to try?" and "This time it's her turn to apologize!"

Thus, little by little the foundation begins to weaken. Then one day she comes, or he comes, or they both come wanting to know what can be done to seal the rift and get things back like they were at the time of their lovely beginning.

Most ministers these days spend hours counseling with couples in some kind of trouble. You can take my word for it, those of us who deal with marital difficulties hear everything imaginable and some things you would hardly believe. To show you what I mean here are a few common and not-so-common quotes from my study-notebook:

"He won't talk." . . . "She never shuts up." . . . "His folks never come over." . . . Her's won't go away." . . . "He drinks too much." . . . "She over-eats." . . . "His manners are atrocious." . . . "She thinks she's Lady Astor" . . . "He thinks every move I make is a sex move." . . . "The only thing she makes is excuses." . . . "He needs a psychiatrist." . . . "She's obviously off her rocker!"

I could go on like this for hours. Sometimes their

problems are trivial. We wonder why they can't laugh. Others are rather simple. With adjustments here and there these breaks are easily mended. But then there are those in which matters have gone too far. There is little to do but weep now. These gaps are dreadfully wide and can anyone close this fissure?

Because this is how it is, I have come to believe that my part as third person at the altar is to say some things loud and clear before we get there. I am done marrying couples who want a big church wedding only because that's how they always dreamed it, or because some member of the family is sentimental, or because everybody who is anybody does it like this. From here on in I intend to say at the rehearsal:

"Except the Lord build the house they labor in vain who build it! Tomorrow this wedding begins with the words 'Dearly beloved we are assembled here in the presence of God to join this man and this woman in holy wedlock, which is instituted of God.' Don't ever forget it. This is no fashion show, nor a gathering of high society, nor a tip of tradition's hat before we adjourn for cocktails. We are coming together to establish a new home where the Lord can accomplish his purpose and establish his plan."

Of course there will be those who wonder "What's bugging him?" If anyone should voice the question, I could tell them what's bugging him. It is the steady parade of those who come with the broken pieces and broken vows and broken hearts.

Like I say, I really do think they meant it when they pledged their love "Till death do us part!" But here they are pointing the finger, blaming each other, excusing themselves, rationalizing, justifying the breakup—

"I simply don't care any more." . . . "My feelings are thoroughly dead." . . . "But you did care once, didn't you?" . . . "You promised to love forever!" . . . "O sure, that!" . . . "But we were so immature!" . . . "We didn't know all the involvements!" . . . "I really don't think it could possibly work!"

They're right. It couldn't. It never could, ever, the way they've been building. The trouble is *no verticals!* Nothing but horizontals. No upward thrust.

This is why I spend considerable time in marriage consultation talking about prayer. In my opinion nothing, and I mean absolutely nothing, matters more than this: Can these two children of God accept the fact that he made them and brought them together to create something not first for themselves but first for him? And if they can believe this then the next question is: "Will you open the channels daily for his spirit to touch your spirits and his love to come into your home?"

I have seen marriages that looked for all the world like they were shattered beyond any earthly power to put them back together. And they were. But some of these are still going on and going greater than ever because they learned to pray. So help me, this is a fact. *I have never known one couple who prayed together who didn't find their marriage moving toward deeper understanding, growing inner joy, and a finer, fuller love.*

There will be days when you simply won't have time for all you would like to do. Almost everyone I know who has a living to earn and a home to manage feels harried and hurried more than he wishes he did. But the truth is that some people do manage to live with a kind of inner calm.

How do they do this? If you were to ask them they might tell you that they don't do it at all. The secret is that everything they do is done from an inner center of reference.

Your home can know this presence and set itself down in this peace. But it won't come without effort. This is why if I were you I would determine that nothing will take precedence over this—that you look to the Lord together at least once every day.

Sometimes it should be an unhurried block of time when you hold hands and discuss what you wish to pray about. Then you bow your heads and one of you prays aloud, or you both do, or maybe even better you pray silently, each talking to God as you understand him. Then there can be other days when you spend only a few moments for the vertical thrust.

The truth is that "How to pray?" isn't nearly as important as "Do you pray?" If you do pray, and pray regularly, you will be led to ways of prayer that are right for you and this is what matters.

So the rule for married prayer is: "We will pray for each other and with each other. Every day we will pray and the more we have to do the more we will remember to pray!"

Sure there are homes where God is left out and they never pray and still they hold together. I'm glad that's true. It is obvious that we need permanency of every kind. But from what I've seen this truth holds: *The kind of homes we most need are those where two lives are being drawn together by a holy love greater than their own.*

So we hope your tea leaves read well, and your

crystal ball looks good, and the sign of your stars is promising. We wish you smooth sailing, calm waters, *bon voyage*. May fortune smile. May you have good luck.

All these we want for you and Marilyn plus every other happy hope the human mind could possibly concoct. But if, as so often is true, we would need to limit our wishes, then the one great wish we have for you is that you may learn to be open to Divine love.

Actually the truth is that God never quits loving. He's there one hundred percent of the time, knocking, waiting, hoping.

In the light of this truth, what any marriage needs is to keep in tune with the Infinite. When you do your part, he does his. And what he does is to draw your love to his in a sacred triune relationship.

Those who have experienced this can tell you there is no greater love.

Prayerfully,
Dad

The Twenty-ninth Letter:

THE MAN WHO HAD A "THING" ABOUT GUNS

Dear Phil,

I used to hunt ducks with a man who had a "thing" about his guns. He also had a "thing" about my gun. He polished his with some special kind of oil, which smelled like bananas. And he ate me out in the blind whenever the ducks weren't flying because my gun didn't smell like bananas. In fact, my gun even had some scratches on the brown part. It also had some terrible stuff called "pitting" in the barrel and he said this was because I didn't clean it first thing when I got home after a hunt.

But there were some good reasons why I kept hunting with this firearm perfectionist. He was a member of the best duck lease on the river and I wasn't. He was also chairman of the board at our church and we could talk business to and fro. The third reason wasn't so good. He was having trouble with his wife and I hoped we might be able to save the marriage.

But we couldn't. Finally, she gave up. They got a divorce. It was one of those cases that would make a grown man cry. There he would sit in his beautiful den—antelope heads, stuffed pheasants, lush white rug made from the hide of a mountain goat, cabinet full of beautiful guns all polished with oil that smelled like bananas.

He would stand there by the case taking them out and handling them with tender, loving care. Then he would remember the way my gun looked and take off again on one of his diatribes about the care of guns. This never failed to shame me and I would go home determined to get out my gun and clean it like it had never been cleaned before.

But do you know what happened? When I arrived home, she would be waiting for me at the door. So we would sit down on our rocking love seat, hold hands, visit, and like that. In less time than it takes to look into her eyes, I completely forgot my noble resolve to love my gun with more devotion.

The other day as I was thinking back on all this, a great idea occurred to me. Funny, isn't it, how we so often get these brilliant thoughts too late?

What happened was that my banana-oil brother would *always* include in his lectures at least one reference like this: "I just can't understand how a man could invest so much in a gun and then let it go to pot!"

The thought that came to me was, "Why didn't I figure up how much it cost him to get his wife? Courtship expenses—movies, flowers, dinners, gifts, postage, the wedding. All the food she's eaten through the years, clothes she's bought, medicine. It really would be a tidy sum, wouldn't it?"

Then I could have said "My dear Whoozit! You are absolutely right! Let us now turn your brilliant observation to other things. Isn't a man a fool to invest so much in marriage and then let it go to pot?"

He sure would be, wouldn't he?

Carry on,
Dad